Text by
Federica Magrin

Illustrations by
Laura Brenlla

ATLAS OF
MONSTERS
AND
GHOSTS

TABLE OF CONTENTS

INTRODUCTION TO MONSTERS AND GHOSTS

GOOD TO SEE YOU, FRIEND! You must be wondering who I am. Well, despite looking like a schoolteacher, I am actually a monster hunter and, if I may say so myself, one of the most famous of my kind. My name is **Van Helsing**.

If you are reading this, it means you are interested in the **terrifying world of monsters and ghosts**. To start, don't listen to other so-called experts who traipse around brandishing sophisticated, powerful weapons; the most important thing when dealing with these creatures is not technology, but intelligence. After all, that's how I beat my mortal enemy, **Count Dracula**. And I'm not talking about some tiny, silly monster . . . but the **lord of all vampires!**

In fact, don't believe for one second that **garlic** and **holy water** are all you need to beat this evil, bloodthirsty fiend, as others may say! Trust me, what you need above all else is a cool head and a cunning mind – requirements when preparing to hunt some of the most **horrible** and **frightening** creatures known to humankind.

For the journey you are about to embark on in the following pages – filled with vengeful ghosts, restless spirits and the most bloodcurdling, terrifying monsters – you will need all the courage you can muster . . . and even a touch of madness!

HOW TO READ THIS BOOK

THIS BOOK IS DIVIDED INTO SECTIONS. Each one relates to a certain part of the world and includes a map with the various creatures marked to help you locate them.

You'll find descriptions of these monsters: some are brief, summarising only the most important facts; others are more detailed, explaining the precise locations of sightings, characteristics that make them so infamous, and methods for how to beat them. Some of the most important monsters – significant either for their fame or cruelty – have two pages dedicated to them, with more detailed information on where they live and curious legends about their existence.

READY FOR AN ADVENTURE?
Then turn the page and
prepare to fight!

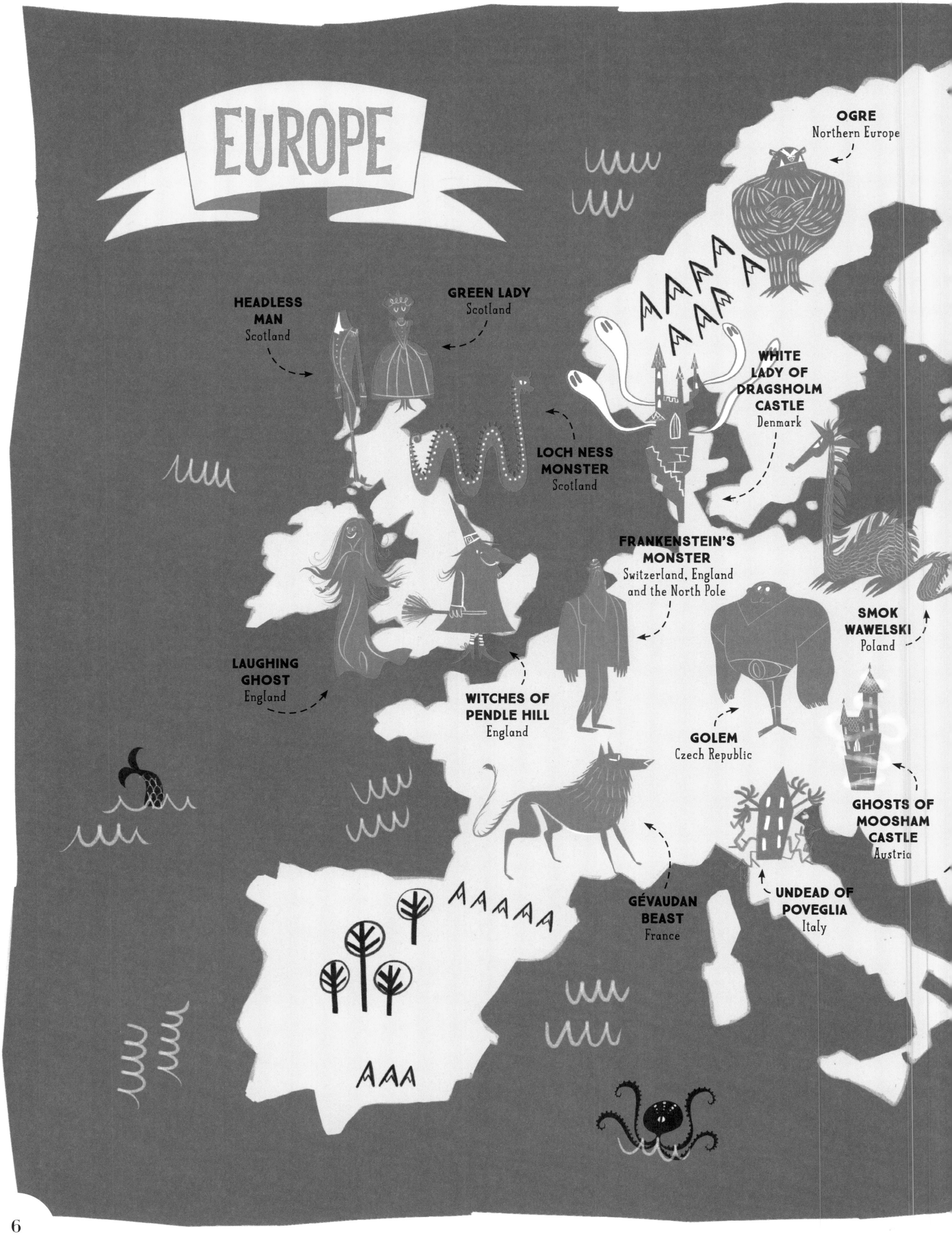

EUROPE

OGRE
Northern Europe

HEADLESS MAN
Scotland

GREEN LADY
Scotland

WHITE LADY OF DRAGSHOLM CASTLE
Denmark

LOCH NESS MONSTER
Scotland

FRANKENSTEIN'S MONSTER
Switzerland, England and the North Pole

SMOK WAWELSKI
Poland

LAUGHING GHOST
England

WITCHES OF PENDLE HILL
England

GOLEM
Czech Republic

GHOSTS OF MOOSHAM CASTLE
Austria

GÉVAUDAN BEAST
France

UNDEAD OF POVEGLIA
Italy

GOBLIN
Caves throughout
Europe

DRACULA
Transylvania
(Romania)

TROLL
Caves near water
throughout
Europe

HEADLESS MAN

WHERE: Edinburgh Castle in Scotland

CHARACTERISTICS: This spirit is often seen desperately searching for his head, which he lost halfway through the 17th century. Along with this ghost, many other spirits live in this ancient castle: a cook, a woman thought to have been a witch during her lifetime, and even a dog. There are so many spectres that you may not be able to visit the castle without being bothered by at least one!

HOW TO BEAT IT: Since he can't see you, he probably won't know you're there, so there's nothing to fear. However, you may end up feeling sorry for him and decide to go looking for his head. Don't do it! There are so many ghosts in this castle that you may find some of the ghastlier ones.

THE GREEN LADY

WHERE: Castle of Mey in Scotland

CHARACTERISTICS: The spirit that haunts this castle has been named the Green Lady. She looks like a sad little girl, and in fact, her death hides a tragic love story. If you meet her, give her a smile. It won't change her fate, but it will certainly cheer her up.

LOCH NESS MONSTER

WHERE: Loch Ness, Scotland

CHARACTERISTICS: The creature that lives in Loch Ness – sometimes called Nessie – is a rather curious monster. It has a massive body, a long snake-like neck, a tiny head, and fins. It's good at swimming and is rumoured to be able to slither on dry land, too.

HOW TO BEAT IT: All the photos taken of Nessie show it swimming, so if you want a close encounter, you'll need to board a boat. This isn't a good idea though, because the monster is big and aggressive. Even if it hasn't hurt anyone recently, in 565 AD, a monk wrote about the funeral of a man killed by the "loch monster", which was the first reported sighting of Nessie. Better not risk it!

THE WITCHES OF PENDLE HILL

WHERE: England

CHARACTERISTICS: There is a dark presence at the top of Pendle Hill. It's believed to be the 12 ghosts of accused witches who once lived in the area, until they were executed. They are seeking revenge, so before trespassing on their land, make sure you have an amulet to protect yourself from their tricks.

LAUGHING GHOST

WHERE: Chambercombe Manor, England

CHARACTERISTICS: This spectral female figure often appears before visitors of the Manor. She isn't scary — on the contrary, she comforts those who see her. She doesn't have a disturbing presence or a terrifying scream like other ghosts. In fact, she usually welcomes people with a sweet smile.

HOW TO BEAT IT: You don't have to! She's a friendly ghost, not harmful at all, which is why you might want to visit her in person. If you're lucky, she'll simply appear while you are there, or you could go looking for "cold spots" — places where the temperature drops, indicating the presence of a spectral entity. There seem to be several in Chambercombe.

THE GÉVAUDAN BEAST

WHERE: France

CHARACTERISTICS:
The Gévaudan Beast looks like a wolf, but bigger, and is thirsty for human blood. Apparently, it's impossible to kill it, and as strange as it may seem, it fears cows. It may be helpful to bring one with you when travelling through France!

GOLEM

WHERE: Old-New Synagogue in Prague, Czech Republic

CHARACTERISTICS: This monster looks like a giant man made of clay and is ready to mindlessly obey its creators . . . no matter what. Although it is surprisingly strong, it has no brain and cannot feel emotions. Would you like to create something like this? If so, you would need a special knowledge of Jewish Kabbalah (teachings reserved only for a small group of religious followers).

HOW TO BEAT IT: Golems are incredibly strong and nearly indestructible. If you get in one's way while it's following orders from its maker, it will crush you like a bug. However, there seems to be one way to stop it: on its forehead, write the Hebrew word for "dead". The only problem is reaching up that high! You will certainly need a ladder.

UNDEAD OF POVEGLIA

WHERE: Italy

CHARACTERISTICS:
This island is said to be overrun by tortured souls, looking for people to terrify. In centuries past, people sick with the plague were sent here to die, and later, a mental hospital was built on this same land. If you want to test your courage, Poveglia is the island for you!

GHOSTS OF MOONSHAM CASTLE

WHERE: Austria

CHARACTERISTICS:
Moosham Castle is home to hundreds of witches' ghosts, all looking for vengeance. As if this weren't enough, apparently there are a number of werewolves in the area, too. A very troubling place – only for the very brave to enter.

GOBLIN

WHERE: Underground caves throughout Europe

CHARACTERISTICS: It looks like a little man, but much smaller. Its skin ranges from brown to red, and it has a pointy nose, chin and ears. Not only is it nasty, it is also diabolically cunning. Goblins are not very strong, but a goblin may try to tempt you with a treat and then ambush you with its friends. And when they are in a group, they are even creepier!

HOW TO BEAT IT: If you see a small, strangely coloured creature that promises to give you something you've been wanting for a long time if you follow it, don't trust it! It may be a goblin trying to trick you. It would never challenge you one-on-one, so all you'd have to do is push it out of the way. But if you end up following it, you may find yourself faced with an army of goblins – and in that case, there is little you can do but call for help.

SMOK WAWELSKI

WHERE: Poland

CHARACTERISTICS:
Smok Wawelski is a dragon that lives in a cave at the foot of Wawel Hill in Kraków. This cruel, powerful being loves destroying anything that gets in its way. Fortunately, it can be defeated: legend has it that a young boy once knocked it out with sulfur powder.

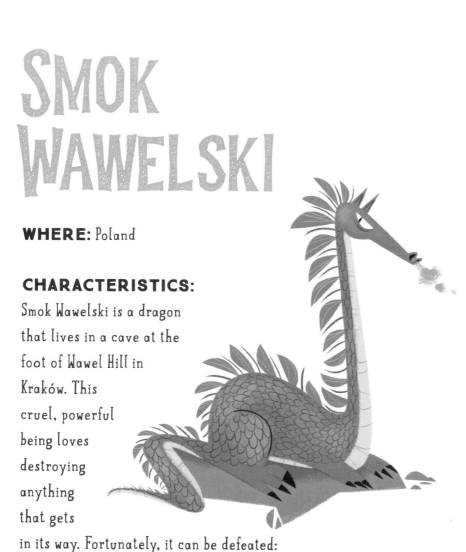

THE WHITE LADY OF DRAGSHOLM CASTLE

WHERE: Denmark

CHARACTERISTICS:
The White Lady is not the only phantom that haunts Dragsholm Castle. If you go to this palace, you should also expect to meet the Grey Lady, the Earl of Bothwell on horseback, some monks, armoured figures, and many, many more ghosts. It's impossible *not* to see them!

TROLL

WHERE: Caves near water and dark forests throughout Europe

CHARACTERISTICS: Ugly and boorish, it has an enormous, wart-covered nose and a bristly tail. It has a violent nature, and it loves playing nasty tricks on people. Although it is very strong, it does have one weakness: sunlight. If exposed, it immediately turns into stone. But let me tell you, don't get too close . . . it reeks!

HOW TO BEAT IT: Focus on outsmarting this monster. It's definitely more powerful than you, and weapons don't do much damage to its tough body. Instead, take advantage of its Achilles' heel: the sun. If you meet a troll by day, run as fast as you can to a clearing. If it's brave enough to follow you, it'll become a rock in an instant! At night, bring a flaming torch with you when entering a forest. The fire won't turn a troll into stone, but it will certainly scare it away.

OGRE

WHERE: Northern Europe

CHARACTERISTICS: Big, strong, grotesque and hairy. The Ogre truly is a disgusting monster. It lives in caves and swamps, and loves hunting people. You can easily beat this brute with a little guile; unlike some other creatures, it's rather stupid!

DRACULA

WHERE: Bran Castle, Transylvania, by day. Flying around in the form of a bat by night.

CHARACTERISTICS: He is the most notorious of all vampires – nocturnal creatures that feed off of human blood. As an *undead* creature, he won't be easy to kill. Pale, with long canine teeth used to suck the blood of his victims, he stays out of direct sunlight and can't set foot in places that have been blessed. Although some vampires have recently reformed, don't be fooled into thinking that Dracula has turned over a new leaf; quite the contrary. He is stronger, more devious and more violent than ever.

HOW TO BEAT IT: Even though Dracula is one of the strongest monsters, he is also more vulnerable in a few ways. He hates garlic, so always wear some around your neck, where he normally sinks his canines. If you find him asleep in his coffin, you could kill him easily by driving a wooden stake through his heart. Another, more complicated way to defeat him would be to lure him out of his castle and into the sunlight, where he would turn to dust. Also remember that he loathes holy water and the sign of the cross.

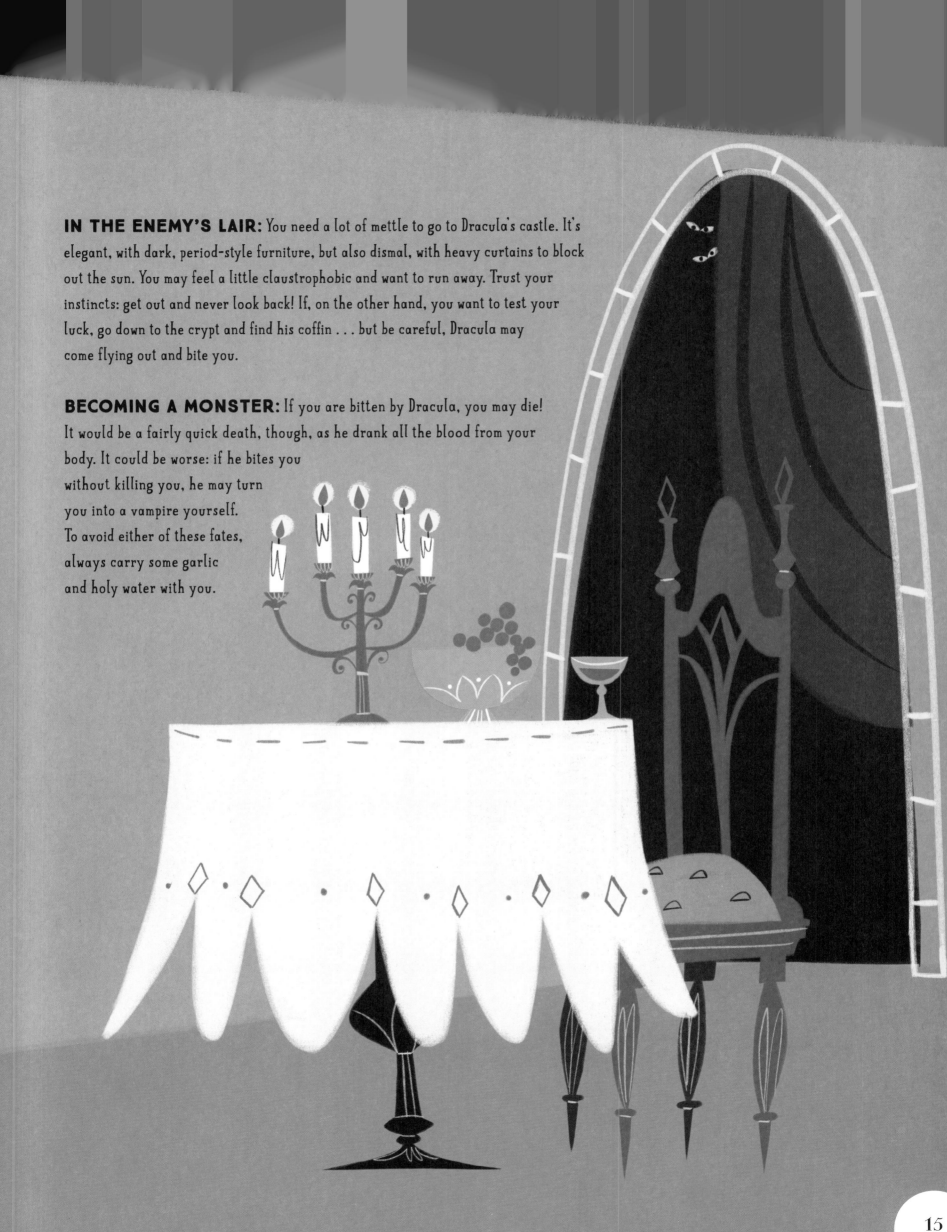

IN THE ENEMY'S LAIR: You need a lot of mettle to go to Dracula's castle. It's elegant, with dark, period-style furniture, but also dismal, with heavy curtains to block out the sun. You may feel a little claustrophobic and want to run away. Trust your instincts: get out and never look back! If, on the other hand, you want to test your luck, go down to the crypt and find his coffin . . . but be careful, Dracula may come flying out and bite you.

BECOMING A MONSTER: If you are bitten by Dracula, you may die! It would be a fairly quick death, though, as he drank all the blood from your body. It could be worse: if he bites you without killing you, he may turn you into a vampire yourself. To avoid either of these fates, always carry some garlic and holy water with you.

WHERE: Drifting between Switzerland, England and occasionally the North Pole

CHARACTERISTICS:
This is a truly monstrous creature. Pieced together from decomposing body parts, he has strips of yellowing skin that barely cover his internal organs, thin black lips, and dead eyes. Covered by grisly scars, he towers over the average-size human. He is also astonishingly strong and nearly unstoppable.

HOW TO BEAT IT:
It's unlikely that anyone would *want* to fight this monster, and your first instinct may be to run away. However, even though he's not known for his kindness, he only acts maliciously because he hasn't been accepted by humankind. If you are sympathetic, he may become a friend rather than an enemy you need to defeat.

THE SCIENTIST'S CASTLE: Burg Frankenstein is a ruined castle on a hill overlooking Darmstadt in Germany. Over two hundred years ago, Dr Victor Frankenstein brought a stolen body from a nearby cemetery to this same castle. One stormy night, he used electricity to bring a spark of life to the corpse, and this horrifying monster rose from the dead. A rather risky experiment, don't you think?

A RELATIVE OF THE ADDAMS FAMILY: Remember the Addams family's butler? Well, if you look closely, you will see that he looks surprisingly like Frankenstein's monster: big, rather clumsy, powerful and not very bright. Even their eyes look the same, not to mention their hairstyles. Maybe they're distant relatives!

HYDRA

CENTAUR

CIRCE

SIREN

CYCLOPS

CETO

GREEK MYTHOLOGY

CARCINUS

SCYLLA AND CHARYBDIS

BASILISK

HARPY

CHIMERA

CERBERUS

PHOENIX

MINOTAUR

IN ANCIENT TIMES, the very heart of Europe was Greece. Great thinkers such as Plato and Aristotle were born here, and Greece was known for its epic poems like the *Iliad* and the *Odyssey*.

This, however, is not a history book, but an ATLAS OF MONSTERS, so I will tell you all about monstrous creatures instead. This region is also highly noted for its fearsome and unforgettable native beasts!

SIREN

WHERE: Mediterranean islands

CHARACTERISTICS: The true, mythological siren is a terrible, ruthless creature with the torso and head of a woman and the bottom half of a bird, with long claws to grab her victims. The sweetness of her song draws sailors near so she can capture and kill them.

HOW TO BEAT IT: If you are sailing the high seas and hear an alluring melody, be careful: it could be a siren. Since it's very difficult to resist her music, you could try the same strategy as the hero Odysseus, who had himself tied to the mast of his ship. Another tactic is to put candle wax or cotton wool in your ears, so you can't hear her.

CETO

CHARACTERISTICS: The sea monster Ceto looks like an enormous whale, but much more ominous. She lives in seas and oceans and her only purpose is to instil terror. She can frighten the crew of any ship, even the largest and supposedly safest.

CIRCE

CHARACTERISTICS: Circe has the appearance of a beautiful woman with no monstrous traits, but you shouldn't underestimate her. This enchantress makes dangerous potions that can turn men into animals! Be very careful if she offers you a drink, and if you can, take the divine herb called moly as a remedy.

CENTAUR

CHARACTERISTICS: A centaur has the body of a horse and the torso of a man . . . and embodies characteristics of both. At times this creature can be incredibly wise, but he can also be very violent and uncouth. Due to his unpredictable nature, don't get too close!

CYCLOPS

WHERE: Remote caves high in the mountains

CHARACTERISTICS: This creature is abnormally large and has only one eye. His main asset is his strength, which he harnesses mostly for metalworking, but he can also use it against enemies if necessary. Also, he's not a particularly clever monster.

HOW TO BEAT IT: If you try to fight him hand to hand, you will lose within seconds! Instead, you should rely on your smaller, nimbler stature and greater intellect. In the past, other opponents have attacked Cyclops's only eye, blinding him, at least temporarily. That'll take him out of the fight!

CARCINUS

CHARACTERISTICS: Carcinus looks like a gigantic crab. It lives mainly in marshland, where it can hide and then jump on its enemy without being seen. Its claws are its most dangerous weapon, so keep away from them, or tie them up with a strong rope!

SCYLLA AND CHARYBDIS

CHARACTERISTICS: Scylla and Charybdis are two sea monsters who live next to each other in the same strait. While Scylla has six heads shaped like dogs' and many snakelike legs, Charybdis looks like a jawless fish, with hundreds of teeth and a huge mouth that sucks things up like a whirlpool. Quite a dangerous duo!

HARPY

WHERE: Between the land of the living and the kingdom of the dead

CHARACTERISTICS: This creature has the body of a bird and the head of a woman. She flies around hunting for possible prey before diving down and catching them with her dagger-like talons, then she takes them to the kingdom of the dead and subjects them to excruciating torture. When you're out walking, always keep an eye on the sky to make sure the Harpy isn't around.

HOW TO BEAT IT: One good defence is to cover your clothes and skin with something slimy. This way, if she dives down to catch you, she won't be able to hold onto you. On the other hand, if your goal is to capture *her*, you could build a gigantic butterfly net!

CHIMERA

CHARACTERISTICS: The Chimera is a monster with three heads: one of a lion (the main one); one of a goat (on her back); and one of a snake (on the end of her tail). She breathes fire and strikes with her serpent tail! The venomous bite kills her enemies quickly. To go up against her, you will need fireproof clothes *and* an antidote for poison.

MINOTAUR

CHARACTERISTICS: The Minotaur has the body of a man and the head of a bull. Because of his animalistic brain, he only listens to his most brutal instincts and is dangerously violent. He is locked in a labyrinth and cannot leave, so you shouldn't come across him unless you actually go looking for him.

HYDRA

WHERE: The spring of the Amymone

CHARACTERISTICS: This is one of the most powerful and dangerous monsters. The Hydra is a water snake with nine heads, one of which is immortal, and it can defeat anyone. All it needs to do is breathe on you, and you may die from its poisonous fumes! Watch out for its blood and footprints, too, which are toxic.

HOW TO BEAT IT: The only one who has ever defeated the Hydra is Heracles. And how did he do it? He started with flaming arrows, then tried cutting off its heads. He quickly realised that two heads were growing back for every one he sliced off. Next, he tried fire, and finally, he squashed its immortal head under a rock. If you're looking for an epic battle, make sure you are as cunning and strong as this demigod!

PHOENIX

CHARACTERISTICS:
The Phoenix is also known as the Firebird because it can be reborn from its own ashes. A majestic sight, the brightly coloured feathers make it an awe-inspiring, mysterious and formidable creature.

BASILISK

CHARACTERISTICS:
The Basilisk is a small but mortally dangerous serpent. It's so potent that with a single look or breath, it can turn its enemies to stone. It can even turn the land it slithers across into desert. If you meet it, don't let its small stature fool you – even if you are bigger and stronger, there is nothing you can do to stop it!

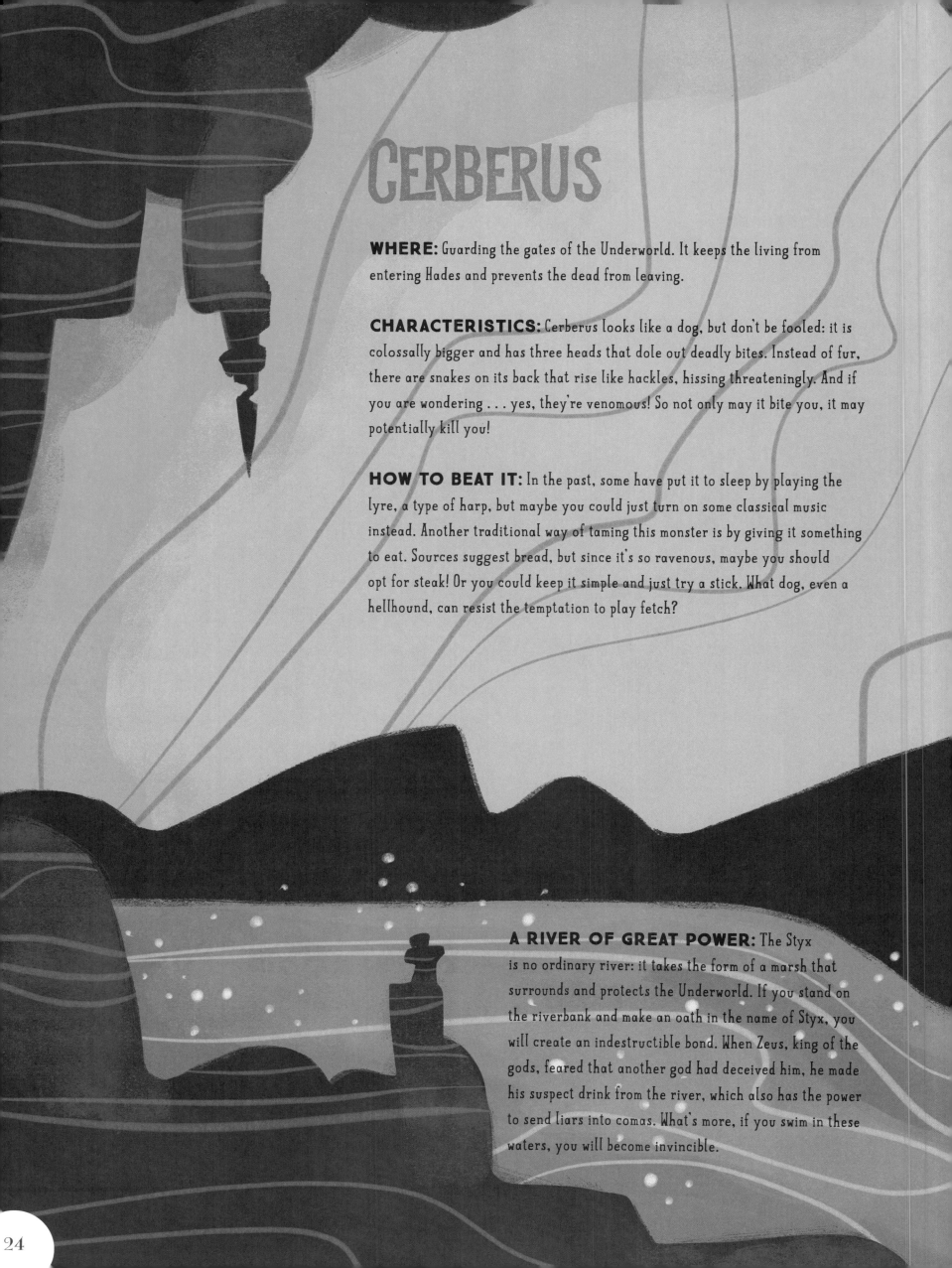

CERBERUS

WHERE: Guarding the gates of the Underworld. It keeps the living from entering Hades and prevents the dead from leaving.

CHARACTERISTICS: Cerberus looks like a dog, but don't be fooled: it is colossally bigger and has three heads that dole out deadly bites. Instead of fur, there are snakes on its back that rise like hackles, hissing threateningly. And if you are wondering . . . yes, they're venomous! So not only may it bite you, it may potentially kill you!

HOW TO BEAT IT: In the past, some have put it to sleep by playing the lyre, a type of harp, but maybe you could just turn on some classical music instead. Another traditional way of taming this monster is by giving it something to eat. Sources suggest bread, but since it's so ravenous, maybe you should opt for steak! Or you could keep it simple and just try a stick. What dog, even a hellhound, can resist the temptation to play fetch?

A RIVER OF GREAT POWER: The Styx is no ordinary river: it takes the form of a marsh that surrounds and protects the Underworld. If you stand on the riverbank and make an oath in the name of Styx, you will create an indestructible bond. When Zeus, king of the gods, feared that another god had deceived him, he made his suspect drink from the river, which also has the power to send liars into comas. What's more, if you swim in these waters, you will become invincible.

A COMEDIC CERBERUS: The hellhound also plays a role in a canto of Dante Alighieri's *Divine Comedy*. In the poem, however, Cerberus doesn't guard the kingdom of the dead, but the entrance to the Third Circle of Hell, where sinners are tortured for Gluttony. Dante's version of this monster has red eyes, a swollen belly and long claws. In fact, here it is even more frightening!

YOU CANNOT CROSS HERE: . . . That's *almost* true! Although the Underworld can't normally be reached by any living soul, many have entered anyway, including Orpheus, Aeneas and Heracles. But how did they get past Cerberus? Orpheus played a lullaby, Aeneas fed it bread laced with a sleeping potion, and Heracles chose a different route: he actually led Cerberus out of Hades!

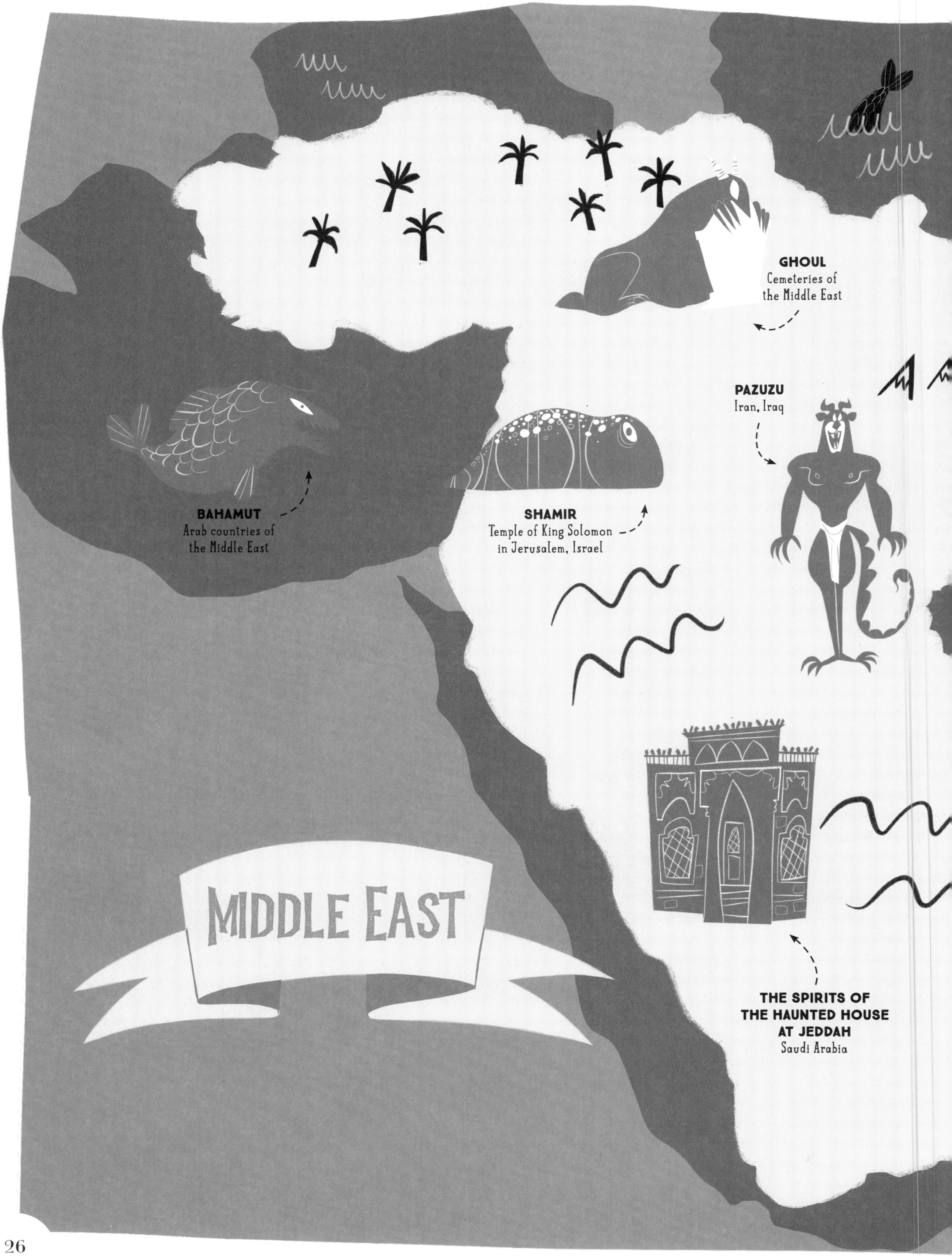

GHOUL
Cemeteries of
the Middle East

PAZUZU
Iran, Iraq

BAHAMUT
Arab countries of
the Middle East

SHAMIR
Temple of King Solomon
in Jerusalem, Israel

MIDDLE EAST

**THE SPIRITS OF
THE HAUNTED HOUSE
AT JEDDAH**
Saudi Arabia

AIL
Afghanistan
and Tajikistan

AZHI DAHAKA
Caspian Sea

HUMBABA
Iran, Iraq

TIAMAT
Iran, Iraq

MARID
Seas and oceans
of Arab countries

KUYŪTHĀ
Arabian Peninsula

AIL

WHERE: The Hindu Kush Mountains between Afghanistan and Tajikistan

CHARACTERISTICS: This feminine-looking spirit has long, flowing hair, skin so pale it's almost transparent, and unbelievably light eyes – you may think she has no irises. You can only see her at sunset.

HOW TO BEAT IT: Undisturbed, she is peaceful and doesn't attack. If, however, you don't treat her with respect and annoy her instead, she will definitely come after you. She can be a volatile, unfriendly spirit, so if she's angry, run and hide. There is no other way to beat her!

KUYŪTHĀ

WHERE: Arabian Peninsula

CHARACTERISTICS: The Kuyūthā looks like a bull with severely distorted features. Picture this: 4,000 eyes, mouths, ears and legs . . . on the same creature! A charging bull is frightening enough, but imagine this dark beast racing toward you. And like a bull, the Kuyūthā is rather aggressive, so never *ever* provoke it.

MARID

WHERE: Seas and oceans around Arab countries

CHARACTERISTICS: The Marid is a very strong type of jinn – supernatural beings found in the Middle East. This creature, commonly known as a genie, also tends to be brash, pompous and hot-headed. Actually, it may be best to avoid the Marid: it takes almost nothing to upset it, and then you'd be forced into a fight you can't win!

HOW TO BEAT IT: You will need to think on your feet because this monster is as smart as it is arrogant. If you know any spells, that's even better . . . it is said there are rituals that can make it weak and submissive. You'll really want to win this face-off, though, because if you do, the Marid may grant you wishes. Not bad, huh?

AZHI DAHAKA

WHERE: Caspian Sea

CHARACTERISTICS: Not only does the Azhi Dahaka dragon have three heads, but it is also incredibly strong and intelligent. Be careful if you cross this monster – its dangerous tricks can fool even the smartest minds on Earth.

BAHAMUT

WHERE: Arab countries of the Middle East

CHARACTERISTICS: Imagine a large fish and then make it even bigger. Ready? Imagine it bigger and bigger, and then you might have an idea of how gigantic the Bahamut is. This fish is so gargantuan that it supports the whole world on its back. Obviously the water it lives in is infinite, and its depths are as black as night.

SHAMIR

WHERE: The ancient Temple of King Solomon in Jerusalem, Israel

CHARACTERISTICS: This giant worm is very strong and can cut through enormous rocks. Although it has the potential for a lot of destruction, its good nature makes it a benevolent monster. It likes helping humans with all types of construction, such as building towers and preparing blocks of stone for monuments. Give it a boulder, and it'll know what to do!

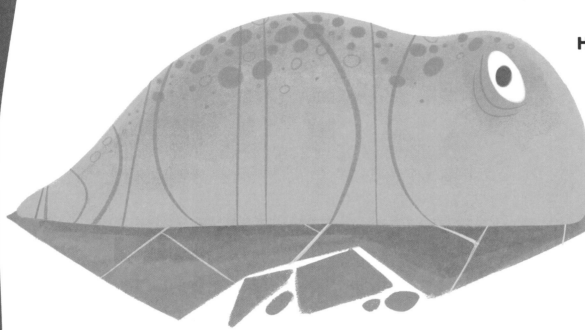

HOW TO BEAT IT: You won't *need* to beat it! Despite its incredible size, it's pleasant and helpful. It's more likely to assist you in making something than deliberately harm you. However, be careful that it doesn't accidentally squash you. If you manage to make friends with it, you'll always have a building buddy.

THE SPIRITS OF THE HAUNTED HOUSE AT JEDDAH

WHERE: Saudi Arabia

CHARACTERISTICS: On the coast of Jeddah, there is a house infested with dark, evil spirits. A flock – or *murder* – of crows has taken over the decaying rooftop. Taxi drivers refuse to go anywhere near it; they all fear the house, and do you know why? Because 16 people have entered . . . and have never been seen again.

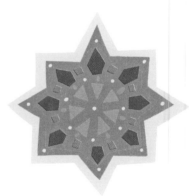

TIAMAT

WHERE: Persian Gulf

CHARACTERISTICS: This deity takes the form of a female dragon with a long, snake-like neck. She is so powerful that she can govern the chaos from which the world came. She is an essence of pure strength, able to beat all other beings. What's more, she possesses the Tablet of Destinies, which give her control over the Universe.

HOW TO BEAT IT: It's hard to imagine a way to defeat such a creature. But there has been one success: the god Marduk was able to capture Tiamat in a net, throw wind at her, and then pierce her with an arrow. Of course that must not have been easy . . . but building a trap to slow her down while you escape might be a good plan.

HUMBABA

WHERE: Iran and Iraq

CHARACTERISTICS: Humbaba is a repulsive monster. Don't you agree? What would you think of a creature with the teeth of a dragon and entrails covering its face? Horrible, right? And there's more: it also has an earsplitting voice that instills fear in humans – and even causes earthquakes!

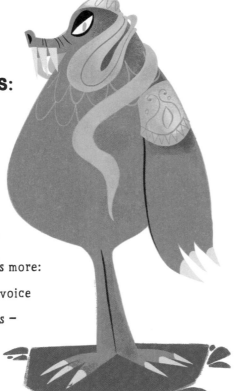

PAZUZU

WHERE: Iran and Iraq

CHARACTERISTICS: The demon Pazuzu is terrifying – with the head of a human, but the muzzle of a lion and horns. He has claws where his feet should be and lion paws instead of hands. Not to mention he has a scorpion tail. If you see him, run: his breath will make you sick!

GHOUL

WHERE: In cemeteries or the remote countryside of the Middle East. It can also take to the skies.

CHARACTERISTICS: This creature is a hybrid: half human, half demon. It may appear as either a man or a woman, and can also shape-shift into a horrible monster. Like a zombie, it feeds off human flesh, but there's no need to worry: it only eats corpses, which is why it spends a lot of time in graveyards!

HOW TO BEAT IT: Since it's half demon, it isn't easy to kill, but you may not have to try – usually it just wants to terrify people as they pass. If you pretend to be scared, it will probably leave you alone. But just in case, you may want to give it a hamburger. This isn't its usual diet, but trust me, it enjoys *all* food and will accept your gift happily.

FROM THE CEMETERY TO THE NOVEL: Ghouls are popular among storytellers, as you can see from the corpse-eating creature in Antoine Galland's translation of *One Thousand and One Nights* and the group of intelligent underground beings in the novels of H. P. Lovecraft. Their corpse-eating nature is what makes them the perfect subject for horror novels, too.

TOKYO GHOUL: This Japanese manga and anime series tells the story of a student who is attacked and – for sinister reasons – has some of his internal organs replaced by those of a ghoul! As the first half-human, half-ghoul hybrid, he decides to join a group of outcasts in order to fight the *real* ghouls overrunning his city.

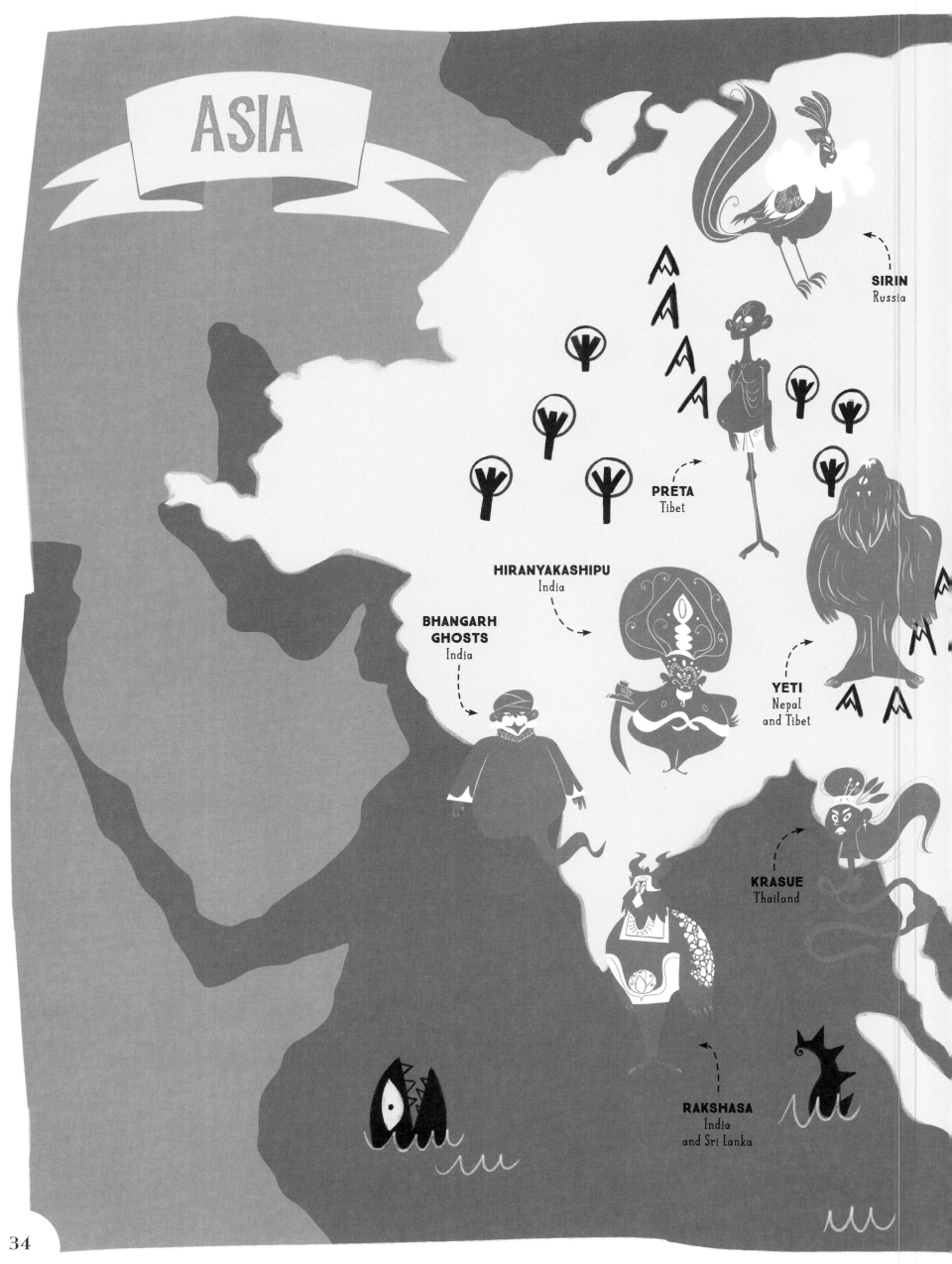

ASIA

SIRIN
Russia

PRETA
Tibet

HIRANYAKASHIPU
India

BHANGARH GHOSTS
India

YETI
Nepal
and Tibet

KRASUE
Thailand

RAKSHASA
India
and Sri Lanka

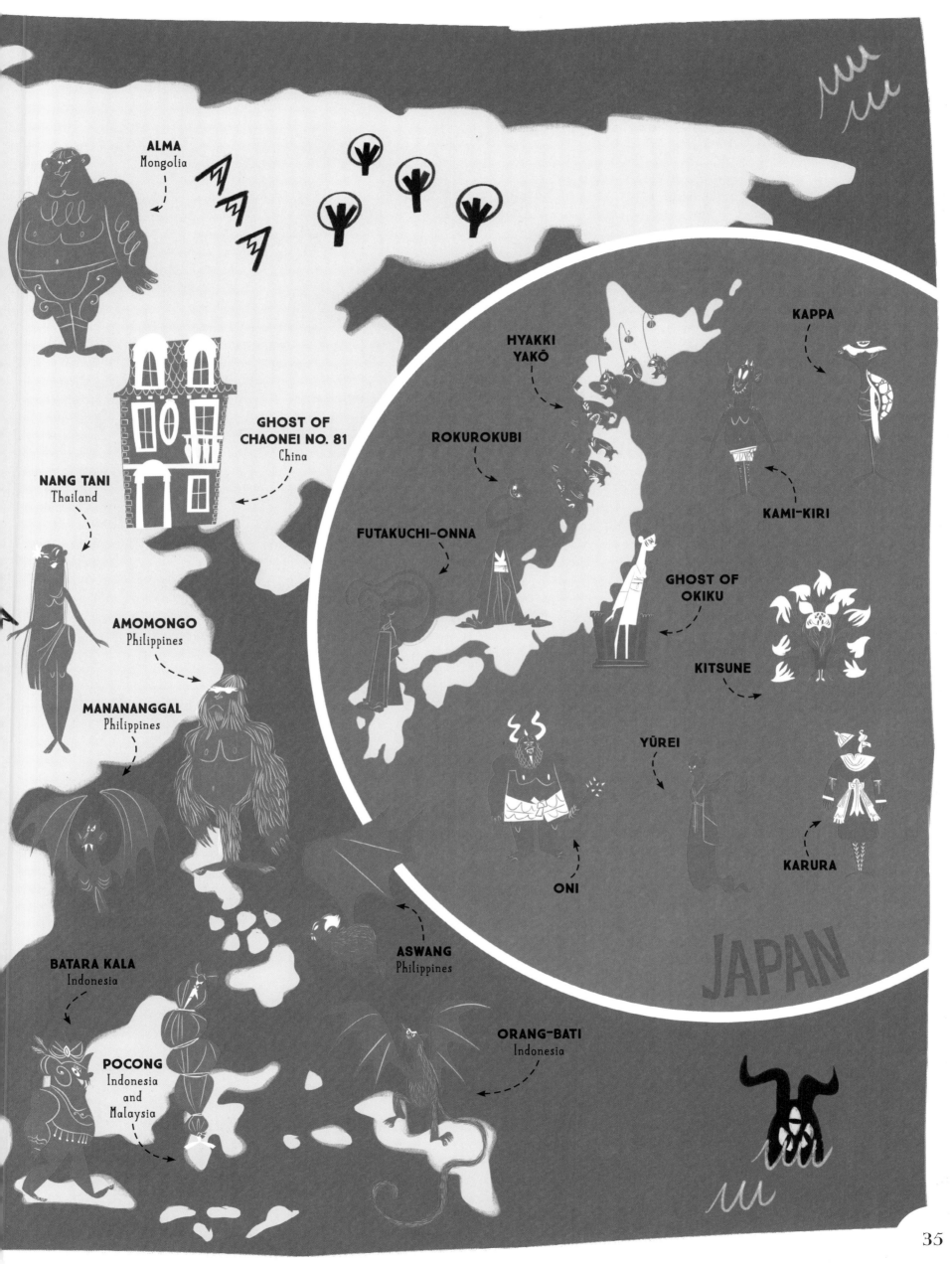

ALMA
Mongolia

**GHOST OF
CHAONEI NO. 81**
China

NANG TANI
Thailand

AMOMONGO
Philippines

MANANANGGAL
Philippines

BATARA KALA
Indonesia

POCONG
Indonesia
and
Malaysia

**HYAKKI
YAKŌ**

ROKUROKUBI

FUTAKUCHI-ONNA

KAPPA

KAMI-KIRI

**GHOST OF
OKIKU**

KITSUNE

ONI

YŪREI

KARURA

ASWANG
Philippines

ORANG-BATI
Indonesia

JAPAN

35

PRETA

WHERE: Deserts of the world and remote regions of Tibet

CHARACTERISTICS: This restless spirit is usually invisible to the human eye and is still paying for mistakes from its life, mostly having to do with greed. As a ghost, it is always hungry and craves disgusting "foods", such as corpses or spoiled leftovers. It has a skeletal body, with a distended stomach and a long, thin neck. Be careful, because it can also cast spells!

HOW TO BEAT IT: It normally stays away from human beings, but if it does come near you, it isn't looking for trouble. No matter what, don't get between this ghost and its food, or it may use magic to knock you out. Also, be prepared for it to appear in front of you out of nowhere . . . just to scare you. Like some other ghosts, if you remain calm, it won't touch a hair on your head.

SIRIN

WHERE: Russia

CHARACTERISTICS: The Sirin has the body of a bird and the hands and head of a woman. She sings with the promise of a happy future, but hearing her music is dangerous. Those who followed her beautiful voice have got lost and eventually died. To avoid a similar fate, plug your ears when she starts to sing!

RAKSHASA

WHERE: India and Sri Lanka

CHARACTERISTICS: In a past life, this demon was a despicable person, and now it's a shape-shifting monster. Regardless of whether it's in human or animal form, it is still vicious and savage. It has a hideous presence, poisonous nails, yellow skin, and very strong teeth. It really is ugly – both in appearance and in nature. It looks for cemeteries to desecrate, people to accost and religious ceremonies to disturb.

HOW TO BEAT IT: Strong, shrewd and magical, it's a very difficult monster to defeat. However, it's said to have problems with monkeys. Every time the Rakshasa fights a monkey, it loses . . . without fail. So make sure you bring a monkey with you – or even more than one – and you'll increase your chances of winning.

HIRANYAKASHIPU

WHERE: India

CHARACTERISTICS:
Hiranyakashipu is more than just a strong demon: he's nearly immortal. He can't be killed by any weapon or living creature. Only Vishnu – who appeared in his half-man, half-lion form – successfully slayed the demon. You have no chance of beating it.

BHANGARH GHOSTS

WHERE: Bhangarh, in Rajasthan, India

CHARACTERISTICS: It is difficult to describe the numerous ghosts scattered throughout the abandoned city of Bhangarh because they are so varied. In fact, legend has it that a mystic cursed the city, causing death and destruction to fall over the land and everyone in it. At night, among the ruins of palaces and temples, you can feel troubling presences and see inexplicable disappearances and reappearances. There are even signs posted around the area warning you not to visit after sunset.

HOW TO BEAT IT: If you're a thrill-seeker, spending a night in Bhangarh is just the thing for you. But be prepared to hear the ghosts' inhuman sounds, feel their spine-tingling touch . . . and maybe even worse! There are so many different ghosts that it's impossible to have the right equipment for handling each of them. So the best thing to do is to only visit the city during the day and ask others to tell you about what happens at night.

ORANG-BATI

WHERE: Indonesia

CHARACTERISTICS: The Orang-bati is a hybrid of a monkey and a bat. It has huge black wings made of a thin membrane, reddish fur and a long tail. Silently, it swoops down to grab anyone it can, carrying them away. Watch out for the Orang-bati!

AMOMONGO

WHERE: The caves of Mount Kanlaon, Philippines

CHARACTERISTICS: The Amomongo looks like an ape but is the size of a human. It's covered in thick black fur and has incredibly sharp nails. It uses its strength to raid herds of cattle and other livestock, and it is not an easy opponent.

HOW TO BEAT IT: Luckily this powerful monster is fairly reserved and tries to avoid contact with humans. Because of its insatiable appetite, however, it does hunt for chickens, geese, cows and any other animal it can find. It isn't wise to come between the Amomongo and its dinner. If you are on a farm and see this monster, hightail it out of there before it can hurt you . . . even by accident!

MANANANGGAL

WHERE: Philippines

CHARACTERISTICS:
The Manananggal is one of the most bloodthirsty vampires in the world, always on the hunt for a fresh kill. He should be easy to beat, however. At night, he flies around with just the upper part of his body, leaving the bottom half behind on the ground. If you put some garlic, salt or ashes on his legs, he won't be able to reconnect with his torso. Goodbye, Manananggal!

POCONG

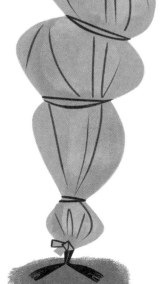

WHERE: Indonesia and Malaysia

CHARACTERISTICS:
The Wrapped Ghost, or Pocong, is a spirit that hops around – still wrapped in the bandages from its funeral. With its feet tied up, it has to jump from place to place as it searches for someone to set it free. There's nothing to fear, actually; if you untie the burial shrouds, it will stop bouncing around haunting people!

NANG TANI

WHERE: The banana tree groves of Thailand

CHARACTERISTICS: On a full moon, this spirit appears as a beautiful woman with long black hair, dressed in the traditional green clothes of Thailand. You can tell she's a ghost because she hovers above the ground, never resting her feet. Be careful: if you cut down a banana tree that is home to a Nang Tani, you will be cursed!

HOW TO BEAT IT: Normally this banana ghost has a good relationship with people and actually wants to help those in need by offering them food. You shouldn't worry about meeting one – unless you chop down her tree. After all, you would get pretty angry if someone destroyed your house, too! When in doubt, never touch a banana tree, and if you know a tree is home to a Nang Tani, bring an offering with you. The spirit will soon pay you back for your generosity.

KRASUE

BATARA KALA

WHERE: Java, Indonesia

WHERE: Thailand

CHARACTERISTICS:
Krasue is an unsightly spirit. She is just a floating head with her heart and intestines dangling underneath. Horrible, right? Well, that's not all. She's ravenous, and will eat anything: rubbish, live animals and even human flesh. Whatever you do, do *not* get in her way!

CHARACTERISTICS:
Batara Kala is a god that looks like an ogre, with a violent disposition and an insatiable appetite. Even more dreadful, he is the god of time and destruction! To avoid clashing with him, take a cue from the people of Java and perform ceremonies that keep him at bay.

GHOST OF CHAONEI NO. 81

WHERE: A mansion at Number 81, Chaonei, Beijing, China

CHARACTERISTICS: No one really knows what this ghost looks like, but it's impossible to walk through the abandoned rooms of this ancient manor without hearing a mysterious noise or feeling a paranormal presence. This ghost is believed to be the tortured soul of a woman who died in the estate, so she amuses herself by terrifying the brave people who step inside her home.

HOW TO BEAT IT: Since you can't see this spirit, it's rather difficult to confront her. You may get chills from a rustling in the corner or a whisper behind you, but when you turn around, nothing will be there except the crumbling walls and broken floor. Remember, she only haunts like this because she is lonely, so let her know that you're a friend. Bring her a gift – a film to watch or some music to listen to – and she won't be a problem anymore.

ALMA

WHERE: Mongolia

CHARACTERISTICS: The wild creature named Alma looks like a savage hairy man. He lives in the arid, uninhabited regions of the Gobi Desert. There are no reports of him attacking anyone, but he's known for his shocking strength – so just in case, it's best to steer clear of him.

ASWANG

WHERE: The countryside of the Philippines

CHARACTERISTICS:
It's a member of the vampire family and can change shape. During the day it blends in as a human, but after dark it becomes a disturbing creature, sometimes a bat, a wolf . . . or even a demon! It has a proboscis-like tongue, used to suck up the blood of its prey. It doesn't usually attack people, but when it does, it travels to other regions where it doesn't know anyone.

HOW TO BEAT IT: Unlike other vampires, it has no problems with sunlight and it's not dangerous in human form. After the sun goes down, however, use the same methods you would for other blood-sucking creatures: garlic and religious objects, such as crosses and holy water. You can also kill it by cutting off its head.

HOW TO RECOGNISE ONE: Although it's easy to see what you're up against when facing other creatures, it's not so easy with an Aswang. Here are some suggestions that may help you:

1. If you see yourself reflected upside down in its eyes . . . run away, it's an Aswang!

2. If the person in front of you has bloodshot eyes from staying up all night, it could be a shape-shifting vampire.

3. If you hear a strange ticking noise, there's an Aswang coming towards you. Be careful though: the closer it gets, the quieter it is!

AN ASWANG AS A FRIEND: It's certainly not easy to trust a monster, but it seems that this one is okay. If it gets to know you, it can't harm you at all, which is why it never attacks in its own village. When it needs to feast, it moves away. Although it may seem dangerous, it's actually best to have one as your neighbour!

YETI

WHERE: The Himalayan mountain range, between Nepal and Tibet

CHARACTERISTICS: The Yeti is a bit like a person, but much bigger and furrier. It's also up to 10 feet tall and covered in thick, silvery-white fur. Preferring the wildest places of the highest mountains, it feeds on lichen and other plants, and only attacks to defend itself.

HOW TO BEAT IT: The problem isn't so much how to fight it, but how to *find* it. It lives in an incredibly remote place and avoids contact with other animals. Since it loves lichen, you may try putting some in a spot where it's already been seen. But if it falls into your trap, just take a picture of it. If it gets angry, it's so strong it could rip you to shreds!

WHO'S "ABOMINABLE"?: Sometimes the Yeti (meaning "that thing there") is called the Abominable Snowman. This is due to a mistranslation of the local term Metoh Kangmi, meaning "man-bear snowman". In fact, in the areas where the Yeti lives, there are three different types: Nyalmot, the largest; Rimi, about the size of a person; and Raksi-Bombo, which is tiny.

TRAVELLING MONSTER: Based on sightings, which have happened almost everywhere along the Himalayan range, the Yeti seems to love moving around. Some people even claim to have seen it along the Altai mountain range, which runs through China, Mongolia, Russia and Kazakhstan, but most people have seen it between Nepal and Tibet. It seems to prefer being in areas above 5,000 metres, where there are glaciers and lots of rocks to hide behind.

JAPANESE MONSTERS

KAMI-KIRI

CHARACTERISTICS: The Kami-kiri is a sort of mischievous imp who enjoys tricking his unsuspecting victims by cutting their hair without their consent. This is why its hands are shaped like scissors. The Kami-kiri comes out at night and, under the shroud of darkness, breaks into people's homes and . . . snip-snip! It cuts a lock of hair, sometimes more. As long as you don't mind wearing your hair short, you have nothing to fear from this monster.

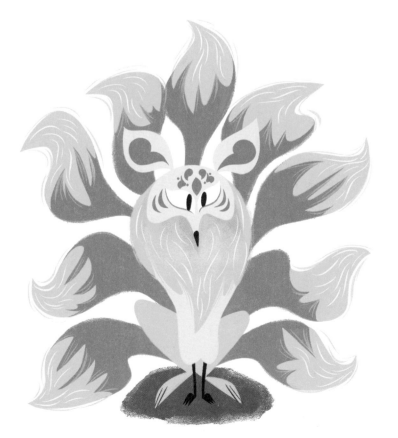

KITSUNE

CHARACTERISTICS: The Kitsune is a fox with supernatural powers that can turn itself into a human being whenever it wants. Its magic becomes stronger as it gets older. To find out how old it is – and how much power you'll need to beat it – just count its tails. The maximum is nine!

ROKUROKUBI

CHARACTERISTICS: The Rokurokubi looks like a normal human being until nighttime, when it stretches out its disturbingly long neck. It's not usually violent, but it still enjoys frightening passers-by; it stands in front of them and extends its neck like a twisted bobblehead. If you're not expecting it, it's normal to be creeped out!

KAPPA

CHARACTERISTICS: The Kappa is an aquatic monster with webbed feet, a tortoise shell on its back, and a monkey-like frame. Another special characteristic is also its greatest weakness: an indentation on the top of its head that is filled with water. If the water spills, the Kappa loses its supernatural powers. If someone bows to the Kappa, it must bow back, but by doing so, it drops the water!

HYAKKI YAKŌ

CHARACTERISTICS: The Hyakki Yakō is a procession of a hundred demons that come out at night in the summer. If you're near the procession, you may die instantly, even if none of the ghosts disturb you directly. In order to watch the parade safely, you need to be protected by a sacred ritual.

GHOST OF OKIKU

CHARACTERISTICS: The Ghost of Okiku looks like a long-haired girl dressed in white, and she slithers out of the well near Himeji Castle. She seeks revenge against the samurai who tortured and killed her. The problem is, the samurai is also dead now, so all she can do is torment innocent visitors to the castle.

ONI

CHARACTERISTICS: A kind of orc with multicoloured skin and huge horns on its head, the Oni certainly doesn't look like a monster you can joke around with. What's more, it's ferocious and carries a punishing, studded club called a kanabō . . . so maybe it's better to leave this one alone!

KARURA

CHARACTERISTICS: The Karura is a monster with the body of a man and the head of a bird, and it breathes fire from its beak. Its arch-enemies are snakes and dragons, but since you are neither of these, you should have nothing to fear from this creature.

FUTAKUCHI-ONNA

CHARACTERISTICS: The Futakuchi-onna appears to be a normal woman. However, she has another mouth on the back of her head that uses locks of hair as hands to eat. Some advice: never stand behind a Futakuchi-onna! She may bite you when you least expect it!

YŪREI

CHARACTERISTICS: The Yūrei is a restless soul that roams the world of the living and cannot move on. It has long black hair and is usually still wearing the white burial kimono from its funeral, which drapes over its legs. It appears to have no feet and floats in the air. There are a number of types of Yūrei, from the Onryō, which search for revenge after death, to the Gaki, a spirit that is constantly famished.

AFRICA

MOKELE-MBEMBE
Democratic Republic
of the Congo

ANANSI
Mauritania
and Nigeria

AISHA
QANDISA
Morocco

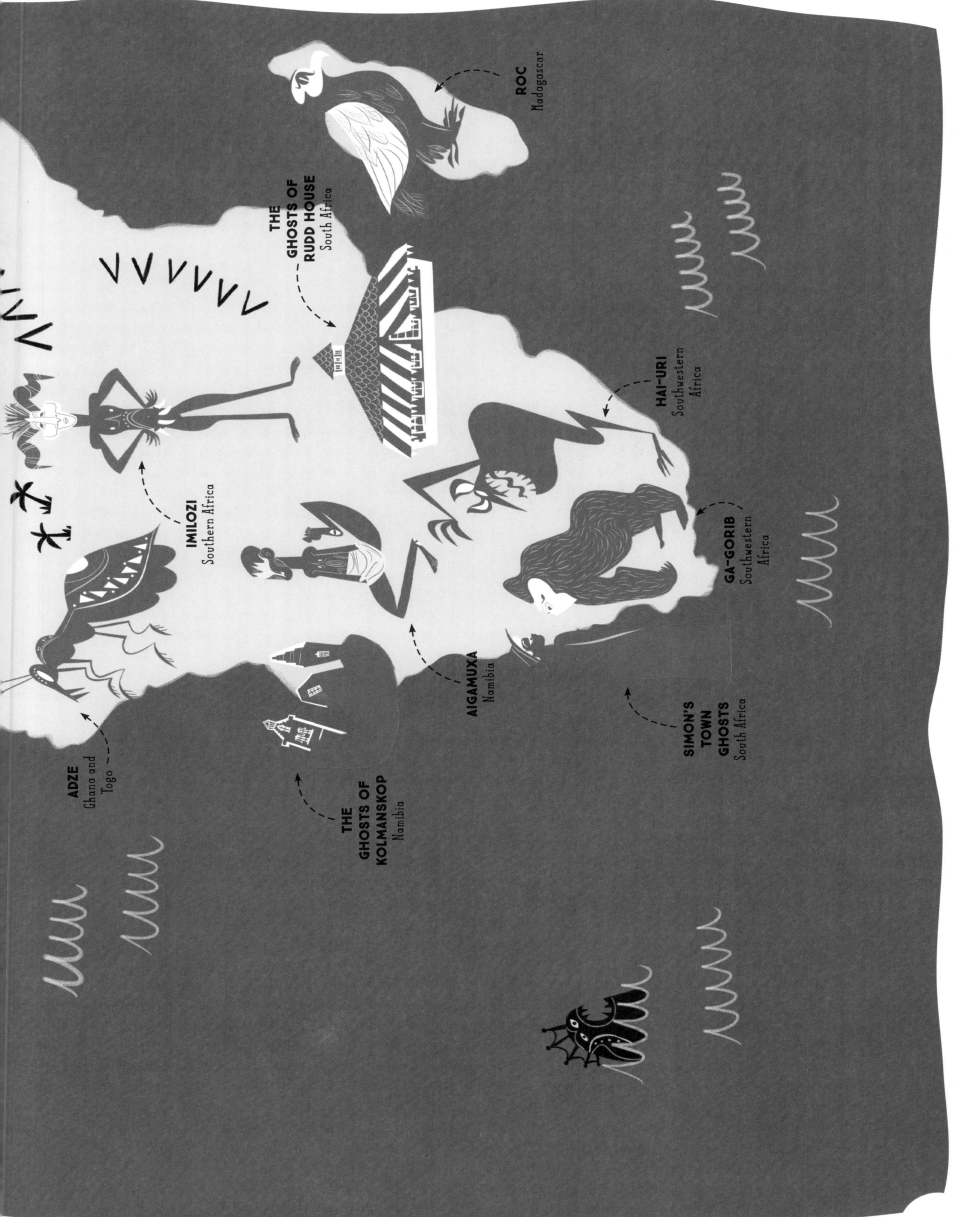

ROC
Madagascar

THE GHOSTS OF RUDD HOUSE
South Africa

HAI-URI
Southwestern Africa

IMILOZI
Southern Africa

GA-GORIB
Southwestern Africa

AIGAMUXA
Namibia

SIMON'S TOWN GHOSTS
South Africa

ADZE
Ghana and Togo

THE GHOSTS OF KOLMANSKOP
Namibia

ANANSI

WHERE: West Africa, from Mauritania to Nigeria

CHARACTERISTICS: This god is half man, half spider and according to folklore, the creator of the world. He also controls the rain and is seen as a benevolent hero who teaches humans how to cultivate the land. However, he's also a cunning trickster. Don't trust him too much . . . you might regret it!

HOW TO BEAT IT: The Anansi rarely fights humans and tries to help them instead. But if you end up on his bad side, try to outsmart him. How? Well, long ago, he was beaten by a sticky, messy, gooey decoy. Confused by the creature that looked like a child, Anansi grabbed the mess and kept touching it, over and over. Before long, he was covered in tar. His limbs were glued together and he couldn't move. Now that's a prank!

AISHA QANDIŠA

WHERE: Morocco

CHARACTERISTICS: Aisha Qandiša is a spirit, or jinn, that looks like a beautiful woman dressed in white. She usually lurks near rivers or streams. So how can you recognise her? As soon as she lifts up the bottom of her dress, you'll see . . . camel hooves!

IMILOZI

WHERE: Southern Africa

CHARACTERISTICS: If you're in Africa and hear a distinct whistle, it could be an Imilozi speaking to you. This is how it communicates with people: through different pitches and tones. They can even connect the living with the dead using their musical language.

HAI-URI

WHERE: In underground caves of Southwestern Africa

CHARACTERISTICS: This monster has half the limbs you'd expect: only one leg and one arm. Despite this, it moves around easily by hopping on its leg. It's mostly confined to its underground hiding place, but it's powerful within that domain. It can even disappear before your eyes. Talk about an advantage!

HOW TO BEAT IT: The best way is to avoid it at all costs. So if you see any underground tunnels or caves, steer clear! It has the power to become invisible, so it could be nearby and you wouldn't have a clue. If it attacks you before you can run away, take advantage of the fact that it has only two limbs. If you tie them together, it won't be able to move at all. Then you can walk away unscathed!

ROC

WHERE: Madagascar

CHARACTERISTICS: The Roc is a monstrous, legendary bird with large feathers and superhuman strength. Just imagine: it's so powerful it can pick up an elephant in a fight! If you were to climb onto its back, it probably wouldn't even notice.

ADZE

WHERE: Ghana and Togo

CHARACTERISTICS: Although the Adze may look like a firefly, it's not an insect at all – it's a horrifying vampire! In addition to drinking blood, it drinks coconut milk and palm oil.

AIGAMUXA

WHERE: The deserts of Namibia

CHARACTERISTICS: This is a truly bizarre creature with eyes on its feet. In order to see, it has to lift its legs, then it uses its arms to walk. Also, it can tear apart its prey – including humans – with its long, pointy teeth. While very strong, it's not that intelligent. Well, nobody's perfect, are they?

HOW TO BEAT IT: In a fight, you would definitely lose to this powerful savage. Not even a superhero could beat it. You may, however, use its stupidity to your advantage, like a trickster named Jackal once did. According to legend, Jackal covered the ground with tobacco, which got into the Aigamuxa's eyes and blinded it temporarily. Then Jackal ran free!

THE GHOSTS OF KOLMANSKOP

WHERE: Namibia

CHARACTERISTICS: Kolmanskop is a ghost town. It seems to have been lost in time, left to the sands of the desert, and today it remains abandoned and haunted. Here, amidst the ghosts, the perfectly preserved buildings seem to come back to life again.

THE GHOSTS OF RUDD HOUSE

WHERE: Kimberley, South Africa

CHARACTERISTICS: Rudd House is famous for being the most haunted place in the city of Kimberley. You may meet several ghosts in the estate: a woman dressed in white on the veranda; the old owner moving through the rooms; and the servants in the yard. Let's just say that it is impossible for you *not* to see at least one ghost!

SIMON'S TOWN GHOSTS

WHERE: Simon's Town, South Africa

CHARACTERISTICS: Simon's Town is swarming with ghosts – from the mysterious woman to the uniformed captain. Sometimes they retain their appearances from their lives, but other times you can only hear them. They are usually pretty harmless, but you should never trust them because some can be aggressive. The worst is the woman – she once shut someone's fingers in a door. Ouch!

HOW TO BEAT IT: Because there are so many ghosts, you should really find a way to protect yourself from each one. But this would take forever! Since most of them are peaceful, focus on the woman. She is rather mischievous, but only because she craves attention. If you show interest in her, she'll leave without harming you.

GA-GORIB

WHERE: Southwestern Africa

CHARACTERISTICS: Ga-gorib should be known as the "monster of the pit" because it sits on the edge of a deep chasm and dares you to throw rocks at its body. If you do, the stones will bounce off and hit you back, knocking you into the abyss. Never accept the challenge!

MOKELE-MBEMBE

WHERE: Lake Tele, Democratic Republic of the Congo

CHARACTERISTICS: This creature looks like a mix of a number of animals: the body of an elephant, the tail of a crocodile and the neck of a giraffe. Its skin is smooth and its legs are sturdy enough to support its massive bulk. Its neck measures three metres long and it has a relatively tiny head.

HOW TO BEAT IT: As a vegetarian, the Mokele-mbembe is not interested in eating you, which is reassuring. If you are on the shore, it probably won't do anything to you at all, but it tends to attack boats that intrude on its waters. When it does strike, it's most likely out of a fear of being harmed. Its favourite food is a vine that produces white flowers, so if you bring some as a gift, it might see you as a friend and leave you in peace.

AND WHAT IF IT WASN'T A MONSTER?: Some researchers have come up with an interesting theory that Mokele-mbembe is actually a dinosaur that scientists had believed to be extinct: the *Diplodocus* or the *Apatosaurus*. Both are sauropods, the largest dinosaurs to have ever lived, and they also had very long necks. Considering the appearance of this monster, it might make sense, don't you think?

LOTS OF ANIMALS FOR THE PRICE OF ONE: The first person to write about the Mokele-mbembe was a French missionary who spent lots of time in Africa. He described it as a monster with the combined characteristics of an elephant, a hippopotamus, a lion, a giraffe and a snake. Well, one thing is for sure – it certainly is monstrous!

A CREATURE OF MANY NAMES: Its common name is Mokele-mbembe, which means "he who blocks the river", but this monster is also known as:
- "Songo" by the Banziri people
- "Badigui" by the Banda people
- "Diba" by the Baya people
- "Guanerù" in the Birao area of the Central African Republic

BIGFOOT
North America

JACKALOPE
North America

OGOPOGO
British Columbia,
Canada

HODAG
Wisconsin, US

GREMLIN
United States

BOOGEYMAN
United States

**RESURRECTION
MARY**
Illinois, US

**GHOSTS
OF STULL
CEMETERY**
Kansas, US

JULIE BROWN
Louisiana, US

NORTH AMERICA

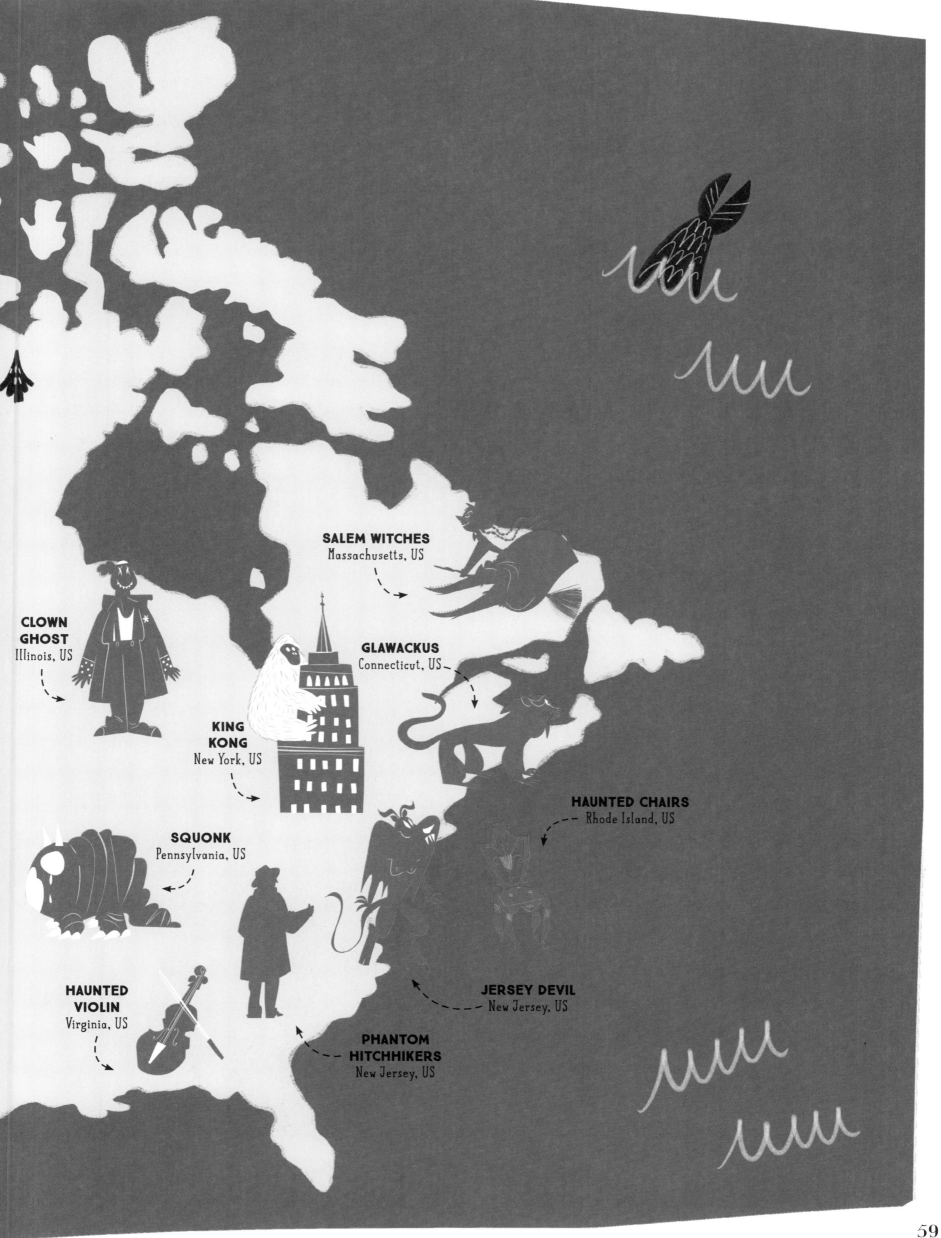

SALEM WITCHES
Massachusetts, US

**CLOWN
GHOST**
Illinois, US

GLAWACKUS
Connecticut, US

**KING
KONG**
New York, US

HAUNTED CHAIRS
Rhode Island, US

SQUONK
Pennsylvania, US

**HAUNTED
VIOLIN**
Virginia, US

JERSEY DEVIL
New Jersey, US

**PHANTOM
HITCHHIKERS**
New Jersey, US

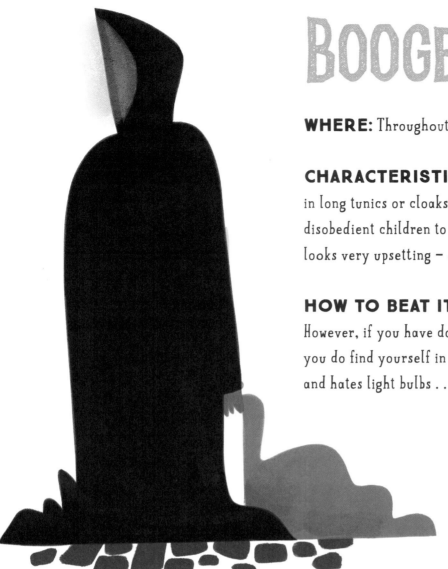

BOOGEYMAN

WHERE: Throughout towns in the United States

CHARACTERISTICS: This being has no specific shape and is often draped in long tunics or cloaks, sometimes with a hood over his head. He hunts down disobedient children to punish them, so watch out! He is known for his cruelty and looks very upsetting – especially because you can't see his face.

HOW TO BEAT IT: First, it would be best just to avoid him by behaving well. However, if you have done something wrong, try apologising to your parents. And if you do find yourself in front of him, turn on a light. The Boogeyman loves darkness and hates light bulbs . . . so all you need to do is flip the switch and run!

GHOSTS OF STULL CEMETERY

WHERE: Kansas, US

CHARACTERISTICS: Dark presences wander the unsettling Stull Cemetery. Restless phantoms love to terrorise unlucky visitors here. What's more – but don't tell a soul – they say that twice a year, the Devil himself appears!

JULIE BROWN

WHERE: Louisiana, US

CHARACTERISTICS: A haunted swamp is creepy enough, but what if I told you that in addition to all of the normal spirits, there's the ghost of a *witch* here? In the marshy bogs of Manchac, the tormented spirit of Julie Brown remains to this day.

GREMLIN

WHERE: Open spaces and homes, sometimes even aeroplanes, throughout the United States

CHARACTERISTICS: With green skin, large ears and no hair, it's definitely not pretty! This creature runs around looking for people to attack with sticks and whatever else it can find. It multiplies when wet and adores getting on planes. Destroying mechanical systems and creating other problems midflight are some of its specialties.

HOW TO BEAT IT: One effective way of getting rid of a gremlin is with light. The sun's rays are deadly to it. If you confront one at night, try not to panic. Instead, convince it to fight in an open space; since there's nowhere for it to hide in plain sight, it might decide to leave you alone. Never get one wet, otherwise you might find yourself face-to-face with an entire army of these creatures!

OGOPOGO

WHERE: British Columbia, Canada

CHARACTERISTICS: In the waters of Lake Okanagan, there lives more than just algae and fish. The Ogopogo also calls this place home. It's a monstrous green snake with the head of a dog or horse. What an interesting neighbour!

RESURRECTION MARY

WHERE: Near the cemetery in Justice, Illinois, US

CHARACTERISTICS: Mary appears as a girl dressed in a ball gown, with elegant shoes and a handbag. She doesn't look like a ghost and convinces drivers to take her to the cemetery, where she suddenly disappears.

HOW TO BEAT IT: Simply by doing what she asks. She is calm and not at all aggressive. She is not looking for trouble; she just wants a ride to the cemetery, so all you have to do is pick her up and not talk to her as she looks out the window. Once you arrive at the cemetery, she will vanish without laying a finger on you.

HODAG

WHERE:
Wisconsin, US

CHARACTERISTICS: What monster is this? It looks like a frog (well, at least its head does), but it isn't a frog; it has claws, a long tail, and spikes on its back like a dinosaur. Strange, huh? It's a Hodag and you better keep away!

HAUNTED VIOLIN

WHERE:
Abingdon,
Virginia, US

CHARACTERISTICS:
What would you do if you heard a violin playing, but there was no one around to play it? Well, if you want to find out, all you have to do is spend one night in the Martha Washington Inn. A hotel for the fearless!

JACKALOPE

WHERE: Forests of North America

CHARACTERISTICS: As you can guess from the name, the Jackalope has the body of a jackrabbit and the horns of an antelope. If you expect to spot this creature easily, you will be disappointed; it tends to avoid people and run away from them. You might hear its call though; it's the perfect imitation of a human voice.

HOW TO BEAT IT: Generally speaking, the Jackalope is timid and doesn't harm people. It could still be nearby . . . just in hiding. It certainly won't ever attack you. However, its human-like voice may trick you into thinking that there is a person lost in the forest. By following it, you may end up off your path. So if you are ever in the woods and hear a voice but can't see anyone, just ignore it!

PHANTOM HITCHHIKERS

WHERE:
New Jersey, US

CHARACTERISTICS:
There are many hitchhikers looking for a ride along Route 37 at Exit 82. But don't stop and *definitely* don't pick anyone up! These aren't flesh-and-blood humans, but phantom hitchhikers!

GLAWACKUS

WHERE: Connecticut, US

CHARACTERISTICS: Beware of the Glawackus! This frightening creature is a cross between a bear, a panther and a lion – and it's really fierce!

SALEM WITCHES

WHERE: Commonly found in the cemetery of Salem, Massachusetts, US

CHARACTERISTICS: These spirits are only echoes of their human identities. Appearing as young women in 19th-century clothing, they float through the air, screaming so awfully that it'll send chills down your spine. They were accused of and punished for practising witchcraft during their lives, and now they seek revenge by scaring the hapless people of Salem.

HOW TO BEAT IT: Try to stay calm, even though they will do anything and everything to terrify you: they will change forms, make revolting expressions and shriek until you jump out of your skin. If you are tough enough not to acknowledge them, they will stop and leave you alone. They only want to frighten you . . . within an inch of your life!

SQUONK

WHERE: Pennsylvania, US

CHARACTERISTICS: The Squonk is a rather mysterious creature. It certainly looks quite horrible and scary, but apparently its main characteristic is sadness. Anyone who has seen this beast says it cries all the time. It appears inconsolable.

CLOWN GHOST

WHERE: Rosehill Cemetery in Chicago, Illinois, US

CHARACTERISTICS: A ghost dressed like a typical clown: wide trousers and a colourful jacket, a fake red nose and a curly, rainbow-coloured wig. He seems harmless and fun; you will probably see him waving, but he hides a cruel soul.

HOW TO BEAT IT: First of all, you have to ignore him. If he thinks he's not the centre of attention, he'll simply leave. But if you acknowledge him and he comes up to you, make sure you have a bullhorn or other noisemaker with you. He absolutely hates loud noises and he'll run away!

HAUNTED CHAIRS IN BELCOURT CASTLE

WHERE: Newport, Rhode Island, US

CHARACTERISTICS: Some inanimate objects have been known to come to life. Take the haunted chairs in Belcourt Castle, for example – it is said that they are haunted by the ghosts of ancient knights. What do you think: is it true, or just a trick?

JERSEY DEVIL

WHERE: New Jersey, US

CHARACTERISTICS: If you come across the Jersey Devil, run away quickly and don't look back. This creature is half human, half monster, with bat wings and a long tail . . . and could swallow you whole.

BIGFOOT

WHERE: The forests of North America

CHARACTERISTICS: Big and brawny, he's covered with thick black fur and looks a lot like a gorilla (but don't tell him that. He might get offended!). He also has gigantic feet, which is why they named him Bigfoot. With exceptional strength, he can hurl you a mile away if he manages to grab you.

HOW TO BEAT IT: With speed and agility. Since this creature is strong but slow, you'll need to move quickly. If you just want to get away, simply run as fast as you can, and soon you'll lose him behind you. If you want to confront him though, just devise a good plan. Bigfoot is anything but smart!

EXCEPTIONAL SIZE:

Weight: More than 30 stone. That's five children, more or less!

Height: Three metres. Two children, standing one on top of the other.

Feet: He leaves footprints that are longer than 60 centimetres. That's huge, considering an adult male's feet are around 40 centimetres.

ROUND-THE-WORLD MONSTER: We still have a lot to learn about Bigfoot, but one thing is certain: he tends to move around, always hiding in forests. As accounts of various sightings throughout North America show, he doesn't like to stay in one place for too long. From the hunter who first saw him in 1840 in California to the woman who stumbled across him in 2006 in Canada, he certainly gets around!

KING KONG

WHERE: First on Skull Island and then in New York, US

CHARACTERISTICS: An ape similar to a gorilla, only much bigger and with human-like emotions: he can suffer from loneliness. Phenomenally strong, he can take down any opponent, including dinosaurs, but he can't do anything against aeroplane attacks. You may see him climbing mountains or skyscrapers.

HOW TO BEAT IT: You obviously won't be able to beat King Kong with brute force, because he is much stronger than even the most powerful human. Don't use weapons! Instead, stop him from fighting by appealing to his human side. In fact, within that great, furry body hides a gentle heart, longing for affection and companionship. If you show him that you are a friend, he might just become a powerful ally rather than a terrifying enemy.

A NEWLY DISCOVERED WORLD: King Kong was brought to New York as a circus attraction, but his life started on a remote island in Asia where prehistoric creatures and primitive beings live among volcanoes and an impenetrable jungle. King Kong is the last of his species and is known as "the King of Skull Island".

THE KONG MOVE: On Skull Island, King Kong goes up against very strong, monstrous creatures: descendants of dinosaurs, such as *V. Rex*. While fighting, King Kong relies on a lethal move – the "jaw-crusher" – where he grabs his adversary's jaws and pries them open until they break.

TOP-FLOOR BATTLE: One of King Kong's most famous battles took place on the Empire State Building. Using his powerful arms, he climbed to the very top of the skyscraper, where he struck out against the aeroplanes sent to destroy him. A truly epic scene!

CIPACTLI
Mexico

LA PLANCHADA
Mexico

CREATURES OF
THE HAUNTED
CEMETERY
Mexico

DOLL SPIRITS
Mexico

AHUÍZOTL
Central America

CHUPACABRA
Mexico, Guatemala,
Ecuador, and Costa Rica

THE
GHOSTS OF
TEQUENDAMA
FALLS HOTEL
Colombia

SARA ELLEN
ROBERTS
Peru

JÉ-ROUGE
Haiti

SIHUANABA
Mexico, Guatemala,
El Salvador, and
Costa Rica

LA LLORONA
Central and South
America

MAPINGUARY
Mato Grosso
do Sul, Brazil

SUCURIJU
Amazon rainforest

NAHUELITO
Argentina

LEMISH
Patagonia

CENTRAL AND SOUTH AMERICA

LA PLANCHADA

WHERE: Juarez Hospital in Mexico City, Mexico

CHARACTERISTICS: Dressed like a nurse from the First World War, she treats and heals the terminally ill. She is kind, patient and selfless, but frightens people by appearing suddenly out of nowhere. Despite the fact that she's dead, she's a really great nurse!

HOW TO BEAT IT: To be honest, don't do anything . . . other than try not to be afraid. If you see her appear and then disappear before your very eyes, don't worry! It's normal. While you should be wary of other cruel and twisted spirits, there's no need to fear La Planchada. She won't hurt anyone; she just wants to help.

DOLL SPIRITS

WHERE: Mexico

CHARACTERISTICS: On the Island of the Dolls, toys don't belong to any children, but to the ghost of a little girl. So please don't take them away, or she might get angry!

CREATURES OF THE HAUNTED CEMETERY

WHERE: Panteón de Belén in Guadalajara, Mexico

CHARACTERISTICS: You'll find anything and everything sinister here. This particularly terrifying cemetery is home to monsters and ghosts of all types: vampires, cursed pirates, devils, ghost hounds, and more. It seems like all the most frightening creatures in the world have found their place amongst the centuries-old tombstones and crumbling chapels in this graveyard.

HOW TO BEAT IT: You'll need a bit of everything, from garlic to wooden stakes for the vampires to crosses and holy water for the devils. If you are thinking of setting foot in this ghastly place, take a suitcase and fill it with everything you can think of. Oh, and don't forget to bring a good dose of courage!

CIPACTLI

WHERE: Mexico

CHARACTERISTICS: The Cipactli is a female creature that looks like a cross between a crocodile and a fish. Remember that she can swim and likes to rip apart everything that comes near her!

AHUÍZOTL

WHERE: Caves of Central America

CHARACTERISTICS: It's similar to a dog or an otter but has an extra hand on its tail, which it uses to grab you if you come too close to it – so keep that in mind. It's also very sneaky – to attract its victims, it starts crying like a newborn baby. Who wouldn't go and check on a helpless infant? It's a foolproof trap!

HOW TO BEAT IT: You have to be shrewd. First, if you are walking through its territory, don't be fooled by the sound of a baby's cries. How? By putting cotton in your ears so you can't hear it! Next, if you find yourself in front of this creature, create a diversion to avoid getting snatched up by the hand on its tail. Always take a piece of meat with you and – if needs be – throw it! The monster will use its third hand to catch the meat, and then you'll have time to get away.

THE GHOSTS OF TEQUENDAMA FALLS HOTEL

WHERE: Colombia

CHARACTERISTICS: Tequendama Falls Hotel: an abandoned hotel on the cliff of a waterfall. It's a creepy scenario in itself. And what if I told you it was haunted? This place is not for the faint of heart!

SIHUANABA

WHERE: Isolated areas of Mexico, Guatemala, El Salvador and Costa Rica

CHARACTERISTICS: She usually appears with her back to you, bathing in a river or pool of water. At first, she looks like a beautiful woman with long hair dressed in white. But beware: appearances can be deceiving. When she turns around, she reveals her monstrous nature. Her head looks either like a horse's . . . or a skull!

HOW TO BEAT IT: If you are ever in this part of the world and you see a woman in white clothes bathing, do not approach her for any reason. But if you forget and you do see her true face, make the mark of the cross in front of you. Apparently she hates that and will disappear straightaway!

SARAH ELLEN ROBERTS

WHERE: Peru

CHARACTERISTICS: The ghost of Sarah Ellen Roberts is particularly frightening because she was executed for being a witch. On top of that, there were rumours during her life that she had been bitten by a vampire. What a sinister spirit!

SUCURIJU

WHERE: The Amazon rainforest

CHARACTERISTICS: It looks like a snake, but is much, much larger. The one spotted in Nueva Tacna, in Peru, was over 40 metres long and 4 metres wide. Just think, that's bigger than 20 men! It eats anything it can find and hunts by wrapping itself around its prey and strangling it, just like a boa constrictor!

HOW TO BEAT IT: This monster is particularly difficult to beat. Since it's enormous and very strong, wrestling it with your bare hands may be fatal for you. So what can you do? Focus on your speed. Its heft makes it slow, so try to escape its grasp quickly. If you do have to fight it, the best thing to do is to find a large, sharp stick. If you can paralyse it at the neck just below its jaw, it won't be able to harm you!

JÉ-ROUGE

WHERE: Haiti

CHARACTERISTICS: Beware of the Jé-rouge! This half werewolf, half vampire is famed for being particularly fierce.

NAHUELITO

WHERE: Argentina

CHARACTERISTICS: If you sail on the waters of Lake Nahuel Huapi, keep an eye out. You may see the prickly spine of the Nahuelito, a powerful monster that's an oversized mix between a fish and a snake.

MAPINGUARY

WHERE: The Mato Grosso do Sul jungle in Brazil

CHARACTERISTICS: This monster looks like a huge, hairy sloth but it is definitely not as friendly. In fact, it has a large mouth full of tapered teeth, and long arms with sharp claws. Thanks to its terrible smell and ear-splitting cries, it can be identified from pretty far away. Strange but true: it only has one eye and it's quite large.

HOW TO BEAT IT: Its fur is bulletproof and there are no weapons that can kill it. Instead, focus on its eye. If you're able to blind it – even temporarily by throwing dirt in it – that'll give you enough time to escape or set a snare. Although, trapping it will only work if you have a stomach strong enough to deal with its terrible smell. . . .

LEMISH

WHERE: Patagonia

CHARACTERISTICS: If you see a Lemish, don't hide in your house. This kind of aquatic tiger has a bad reputation for destroying homes.

CHUPACABRA

WHERE: Agricultural areas of Mexico, Guatemala, Ecuador and Costa Rica

CHARACTERISTICS: As you can guess from its name – chupa, which means "suck", and cabra, which means "goat" – this monster feeds on the blood of goats. I know what you're thinking . . . *yuck!* But that's what it likes! Maybe it isn't so keen on chips! It is a hairless creature, roughly the size of a large dog, with spikes along its back, claws and a long snout to suck things up. It's truly monstrous! Some people also believe it has superpowers, such as mind reading.

HOW CAN YOU RECOGNISE A CHUPACABRA?:

1. You'll see footprints with three toes.
2. You'll hear the peculiar sound of scales rubbing against each other.
3. You'll smell a very unpleasant odour in the air.
4. You'll hear screams that are neither human nor animal.

HOW TO BEAT IT: Since you're not a goat, there's a good chance that you won't be attacked! But if you come between the Chupacabra and its prey, you may be in trouble. Here's a tip: in case it can read minds, as some say, let it know that you're not dangerous. On the other hand, if you want to fight it, perhaps in order to protect a poor goat, try to block its muzzle – its most dangerous weapon – by wrapping a thick rope around it.

MONSTER OR ALIEN?: Some believe the Chupacabra is actually a coyote with a strange genetic disease, while others believe it is an underground creature like a gnome or an elf. According to the most likely theory, it could be an alien. Every time a Chupacabra is seen, UFOs are also spotted nearby.

LA LLORONA

WHERE: Near bodies of water throughout Central and South America

CHARACTERISTICS: This ghost looks like a young woman floating in the air or through the waters of a river. What is most frightening about this spectral figure is the noise she makes – a shriek that could make your blood run cold.

HOW TO BEAT IT: One thing to do is block out her terrifying cries – so maybe try some headphones with loud music! Even better, since her ghostliness comes from her suffering during life, you could try giving her a warm, comforting hug. But there's just one problem . . . she has no actual body to hug! Try some sweets, maybe. Everyone likes sweets.

LA LLORONA AND PAPANTZIN: The story of La Llorona, the crying ghost, brings to mind another famous spectre: Papantzin, sister of the Aztec king Montezuma. This beautiful princess died suddenly when she was young. She was buried with full honours due to her noble status, but was seen several days later as a ghost. It is said that she drifts through Mexico City, crying inconsolably.

THE CRYING GODDESS: In Aztec mythology there is a ghost similar to La Llorona. This is Cihuacóatl, a goddess of the earth, half woman and half snake. What distinguishes her are her inhuman cries and unrelenting sobs. She is often depicted rising from the waters of Lake Texcoco in Mexico, much like La Llorona.

GHOST OF
THE OPERA
Melbourne,
Australia

YARA-MA-YHA-WHO
Australia

RAINBOW
SERPENT
Australia

DROP BEAR
Australia

BUNYIP
Australia

YOWIE
New South Wales,
Australia

THE SPIRITS OF
MONTE CRISTO
Junee, Australia

MULDJEWANGK
Australia

BEECHWORTH
ASYLUM GHOSTS
Australia

GHOSTS
OF PORT
ARTHUR
Tasmania

AUSTRALIA

THE SURRY HILLS GHOST
Australia

HAWKESBURY RIVER MONSTER
New South Wales, Australia

BUNYIP

WHERE: Throughout Australia near rivers, swamps and marshes

CHARACTERISTICS: This grotesque creature looks like a combination of animals: it has the head of a dog, the tail of a horse and the tusks of a walrus. It is also covered with thick, dark fur and has horns. It mainly hunts at night and makes disturbing sounds as it eats.

HOW TO BEAT IT: If you walk past a swamp at night and hear some stomach-turning noises, there may be a Bunyip nearby in search of food. Get out of there quickly so you don't become its next meal! If it catches you, you probably won't make it out alive, unless you are valiant and clever enough to get a muzzle over its head in time.

DROP BEAR

WHERE: Australia

CHARACTERISTICS: The Drop Bear looks like a koala but is not gentle or sweet *at all*. In fact, it unexpectedly drops from the trees where it lives onto people walking underneath, then bites them and runs away. It's mischievous and aggressive, preying on the fact that when people see it, they think it's a cute, eucalyptus-eating koala. Not the case!

MULDJEWANGK

WHERE: Australia

CHARACTERISTICS: The Muldjewangk looks like a merman, only much bigger. Anyone who has fought this creature hasn't survived long enough to tell the tale. Don't worry, though: it is only found attacking swimmers in the Murray River. If you're in a boat, it may spitefully tear through the fishing nets, but that's probably it.

RAINBOW SERPENT

WHERE: In the deserts of Central Australia

CHARACTERISTICS: It's enormous, colourful and breathtaking. In fact, its scales look like a rainbow! According to Aboriginal folklore, this divine spirit was one of the first to appear during the birth of the Universe, known as the "Dreamtime". It can be incredibly charitable, helping humankind, or at other times, merciless and cruel, exacting revenge on those who don't follow the rules.

HOW TO BEAT IT: If you are kind-hearted and well-behaved, you have nothing to fear from the Rainbow Serpent. Its main goal is to shape the landscape, creating the beautiful canyons and ravines of Australia. However, if you disrespect nature and its inhabitants, it will cost you dearly: this snake-like spirit is anything but gentle to people who harm the environment!

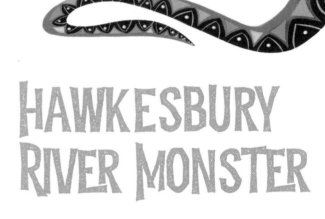

THE SPIRITS OF MONTE CRISTO

WHERE: Junee, Australia

CHARACTERISTICS: In a way, the Monte Cristo Homestead in Junee is a training ground for aspiring ghost hunters. Many harmless (but eerie) ghosts live here, and the owner is a paranormal enthusiast who can give you some useful advice. This is the perfect place to start your first investigation!

HAWKESBURY RIVER MONSTER

WHERE: New South Wales, Australia

CHARACTERISTICS: The monster that lives in the waters of the Hawkesbury River is a lot like the Loch Ness Monster. It has a large body, a snake-like neck, a small head and two pairs of fins. Unlike Nessie, it doesn't like being photographed, so you may be the first to take a picture of it.

YOWIE

WHERE: Australian forests, particularly in New South Wales

CHARACTERISTICS: Quite tall — normally around two metres — and monkey-like, this monster looks a lot like the American Bigfoot and the Himalayan Yeti. It leaves gigantic footprints and is covered in thick, dark fur. Its nose is broad and flat, a bit like a gorilla. As you can imagine, it is also agile and strong.

HOW TO BEAT IT: If you meet one, it will almost certainly run away. It doesn't like human company, so it takes refuge in forests. That way even if someone passes by, it can easily find a place to hide. It never attacks people and is usually peaceful — except, if it's with a cub, then it may become protective. If you show that you're friendly, you can take lots of pictures of it without risking any harm.

BEECHWORTH ASYLUM GHOSTS

WHERE: Beechworth, Australia

CHARACTERISTICS: This former mental hospital is overrun with ghosts of all kinds: not only patients who were admitted here, but also the doctors and nurses who treated them. People who set foot inside experience sudden, cold shivers, a constant feeling of fear, and sometimes even interactions with the dead. Would *you* dare to go in?

THE SURRY HILLS GHOST

WHERE: The rooms of a Victorian house at 139 Kippax Street in Surry Hills, Sydney, Australia

CHARACTERISTICS: This is the spectre of the old owner, whose body was found next to her bed many years after her death. She now plays tricks on those who enter her home. Usually she appears full-bodied, but sometimes she manifests herself as nothing more than mist.

HOW TO BEAT IT: Wear a helmet and pads to avoid being hit by the dishes she launches around the house. She may be the ghost of an old lady, but she still has a lot of vengeful strength. She enjoys slamming windows, ruining the furniture and screeching . . . all just to scare people! Don't let her get to you, though. These are all just tricks, and she has never actually hurt anyone. She's just looking for company.

GHOST OF THE OPERA

WHERE: Melbourne, Australia

CHARACTERISTICS: The Ghost of the Opera, singer Frederick Federici, who died shortly after singing on stage, wanders the changing rooms and halls of the Princess Theatre in Melbourne. There is, however, nothing to fear from this ghost. All he wants is to stand in the middle of the stage so he can receive his final applause.

GHOSTS OF PORT ARTHUR

WHERE: Tasmania

CHARACTERISTICS: There are countless ghosts in Port Arthur. If you ever visit, trust me, you will be inundated by spirits: from the convict who was punished terribly, to the priest of the rectory, to the young soldier. It's as though the city itself is haunted by its dramatic past.

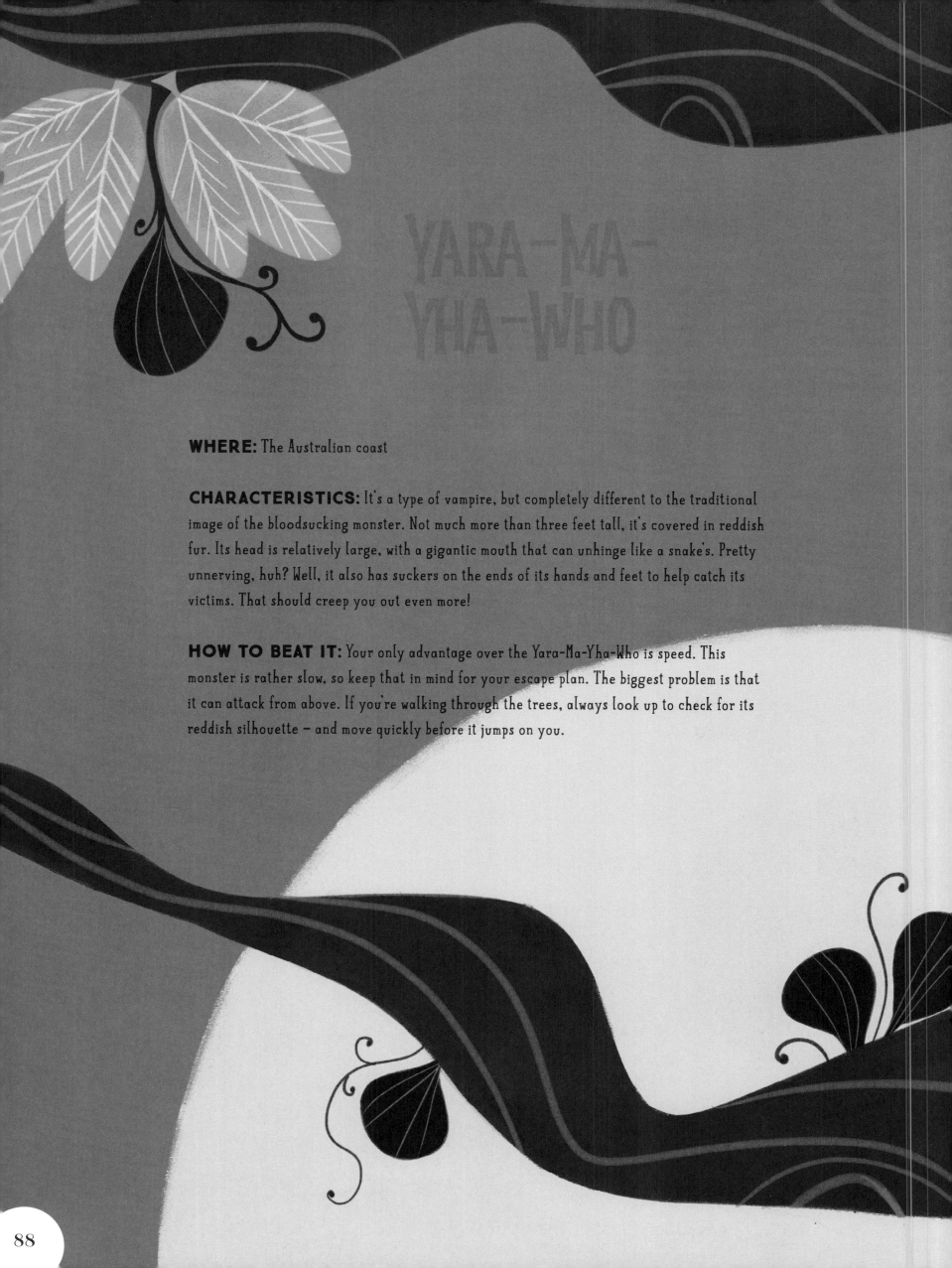

YARA-MA-YHA-WHO

WHERE: The Australian coast

CHARACTERISTICS: It's a type of vampire, but completely different to the traditional image of the bloodsucking monster. Not much more than three feet tall, it's covered in reddish fur. Its head is relatively large, with a gigantic mouth that can unhinge like a snake's. Pretty unnerving, huh? Well, it also has suckers on the ends of its hands and feet to help catch its victims. That should creep you out even more!

HOW TO BEAT IT: Your only advantage over the Yara-Ma-Yha-Who is speed. This monster is rather slow, so keep that in mind for your escape plan. The biggest problem is that it can attack from above. If you're walking through the trees, always look up to check for its reddish silhouette – and move quickly before it jumps on you.

LITTLE RED CREATURES GET BIGGER:
The first thing the Yara-Ma-Yha-Who does when it
catches a victim is drink some of its blood. It then goes
for a walk and comes back later . . . to swallow the entire
body. After a while, it vomits everything up – including
the prey's entire corpse, now smaller and red.
If this cycle is repeated, the victim will
become another Yara-Ma-Yha-Who.

WOW! YOU'VE REACHED THE END!

Well done!

THE LAST CHALLENGE

THINK YOU'RE READY to become a professional monster hunter? Not yet. One last challenge awaits, and some **frightening creatures** are ready to sink their claws into you!

So what do you say? You've battled all kinds of ghosts and monsters. No one can deny that.

It's also true that you've explored far and wide all over the known world . . . but what about the depths of the ocean? **Gigantic creatures** have been hiding in the darknesst there since the beginning of time. Only after you've discovered how to defeat them will you be able to claim you've encountered **all the monsters of our world**.

After that, the only creatures left will be a group of **terrifying ghosts**. They don't move through space, but through time! These are the spirits of famous figures from the past who have journeyed through the ages to terrorise their descendants. Face and defeat them . . . and you will finally be able to proudly proclaim that you are an unbeatable **hunter of ghosts and monsters!**

WATER MONSTERS

KRAKEN

WHERE: The coasts of Norway and Greenland

CHARACTERISTICS: From afar, the Kraken is so big that it may look like an island. Up close, it looks like an octopus or giant squid, but it's stronger than any other living creature. It can use its tentacles – which are the length of a ship's mast – to grab hold of large vessels and effortlessly drag them to the bottom of the sea.

HOW TO BEAT IT: It isn't easy to battle a monster like this, especially if it's angry from being disturbed. It's so strong that no human device can restrain it. If you're forced to fight, your only hope is to use a large harpoon. If you can gouge one of its eyes, you may actually take it down!

A FAVOURITE AMONG FISHERMEN: On its own the Kraken doesn't have a bad temper. Its wrath stems from the selfishness of humans who disturb its underwater lair. Legend has it that fishermen used to be happy to see the Kraken because it would be surrounded by great schools of fish. In that case, the only danger comes from whirlpools unintentionally created by the Kraken moving.

IKU-TURSO

WHERE: Northern Europe

CHARACTERISTICS: Iku-Turso lives in the coldest seas near the North Pole – uninhabited, desolate places – which is lucky for us, since this monster is known to bring illness and death. It has thousands of heads and horns and is terrifying to look at. It is best not to approach it for any reason.

ASPIDOCHELONE

WHERE: Mediterranean Sea

CHARACTERISTICS: So big that it looks like an island you could safely land on, this monster takes advantage of the resemblance to confuse and capture sailors. Up close it has the features of a snake and a turtle. Some advice: before landing on what may seem like an island, throw a stone at it. If it moves, it could be the Aspidochelone!

WHERE: United States

CHARACTERISTICS: Unktehila is also known among Native American peoples as the Horned Snake. It has a long body covered in scales and antlers on its head like a deer. It lives peacefully in large bodies of water, specifically in the Great Lakes. Unlike other monsters, it doesn't attack people; instead, it's an omen of good luck. If you meet one, you have nothing to lose and everything to gain!

LEVIATHAN

WHERE: Middle East

CHARACTERISTICS: This Biblical monster, known as the Leviathan, is the terror of the oceans. It looks like an enormous snake or dragon, it boils the water around it, and it's described as the king of beasts. As the most powerful creature in existence, all other living beings fear it, too. That's why you must always pay attention on the high seas!

UMIBOZU

WHERE: Japan

CHARACTERISTICS: A huge, round head, a repugnant grey body and long, snake-like limbs: this is what the frightening Umibozu looks like as it emerges from the depths of the ocean. It's said to be the spirit of a drowned man, taking revenge on the ships that now disturb its rest. If it asks you for a barrel of water, give it a half-empty one instead – it only wants a full one so it can sink your boat!

GHOSTS OF FAMOUS FIGURES

FREDERICK BARBAROSSA

WHERE: Italy

CHARACTERISTICS:

Many spirits wander through the halls of Oramala Castle, including the ghost of Emperor Frederick Barbarossa. Every year, at the stroke of midnight on December 25th he mysteriously causes the tower to light up. But he's not the only spirit in the palace! You may also hear hoofbeats pounding or weapons clanging – even though there are no horses or knights nearby. A curious place, indeed . . .

ANNE BOLEYN

WHERE: England

CHARACTERISTICS:

The most famous ghost in the Tower of London is that of Anne Boleyn. The spirit of this queen wanders the grounds in two forms: either with her head and body intact, or decapitated with her head under her arm. In fact, it was in the latter state that she first materialised in front of a terrified King Henry VIII. Well let's be honest, you'd be pretty frightened too if you were facing a headless ghost, wouldn't you?

AKHENATON

WHERE: Egypt

CHARACTERISTICS:
Usually the ghosts of famous people are seen in stately dwellings, but this isn't the case for the ghost of Pharaoh Akhenaton. Nomads and tourists say they've come across this spirit in the White Desert in Farafra. He seems to be trapped due to a curse placed on him during his mummification. The priests, irate over the pharaoh's religious decisions during his rule, condemned him to roam without peace in this desert land.

OLIMPIA PAMPHILJ

WHERE: Italy

CHARACTERISTICS: Imagine you're in Rome, enjoying a relaxing stroll at night . . . and out of nowhere a black carriage driven by a ghost crosses your path. This is a common sighting on Ponte Sisto or in Piazza Navona. It's said to be the ghost of Olimpia Pamphilj, who in 1655 fled the city with stolen gold and was never seen again . . . at least not alive!

LENIN

WHERE: Russia

CHARACTERISTICS:
The ghost of Lenin has a peculiar tale. His spirit was first seen wandering the halls of the Kremlin in Moscow – even before he was dead. While the leader of the Russian Revolution was still hospitalised in Gorki, his ghost was clearly seen walking through the Kremlin. There are still appearances today, though usually you can't actually see him – you can only hear his footsteps.

ABRAHAM LINCOLN

WHERE: United States

CHARACTERISTICS:
Many famous ghosts stroll through the White House, but the most commonly seen ghost is that of Abraham Lincoln, 16th president of the United States. He can often be found staring out of the window of the Oval Office, in front of the fireplace or knocking on the doors of the new inhabitants. Basically, he acts as if it were still his home.

AUTHOR

FEDERICA MAGRIN was born in Varese in 1978 and has worked in publishing for over ten years, first as an editor at Edizioni De Agostini and now as a freelancer. She mainly works in children's books, but also writes educational texts and stories and translates novels. For White Star Kids she produced the book *City Atlas*.

ILLUSTRATOR

LAURA BRENLLA started learning to draw at the age of 16, but she grew up holding a pencil. She won a scholarship to study art at Universidad Europea in Madrid, and once she graduated, she specialised in cartoons in a two-year course. Later she was selected to receive digital cleanup training at the prestigious animation studio SPA, where she developed strong drawing skills under the direction of Fernando Moro. Drawing has been her passion ever since she was given her very first pencil.

ACKNOWLEDGEMENTS

Author: Federica Magrin / Illustrator: Laura Brenlla

Published in July 2019 by Lonely Planet Global Limited
CRN: 554153
ISBN: 978-1-78868-346-3
www.lonelyplanetkids.com

Printed in Italy
1 2 3 4 5 6 7 8 9 10

STAY IN TOUCH – LONELYPLANET.COM/CONTACT

Lonely Planet Offices:
AUSTRALIA The Malt Store, Level 3, 551 Swanston St, Carlton, Victoria 3053 T: 03 8379 8000
IRELAND Digital Depot, Roe Lane (off Thomas St), Digital Hub, Dublin 8, D08 TCV4, Ireland
USA 124 Linden St, Oakland, CA 94607 T: 510 250 6400
UK 240 Blackfriars Rd, London SE1 8NW T: 020 3771 5100

White Star Kids® is a registered trademark property of White Star s.r.l.

© 2018 White Star s.r.l.
Piazzale Luigi Cadorna, 6
20123 Milan, Italy
www.whitestar.it